NEW ENGLAND
50 HIKES WITH KIDS

NEW ENGLAND
50 HIKES
WITH KIDS

WENDY GORTON

Timber Press · Portland, Oregon

Frontispiece: A young adventurer hikes through fall leaves

Published in 2021 by Timber Press, Inc.
The Haseltine Building
133 S.W. Second Avenue, Suite 450
Portland, Oregon 97204-3527
timberpress.com

Printed in China

Text design by Hillary Caudle and Sarah Crumb
Cover design and illustration by Always With Honor
Inside cover map by David Deis

ISBN: 978-1-64326-001-3

A catalog record for this book is available from the Library of Congress.

To my mother, Ginny, whose practical support is the backbone of all my adventures and whose trust in independence grew the adventurer in me.

CONTENTS

PREFACE

New England—a collection of six proud states filled with breathtaking views and adventures matched only by the delicious food and rich history you'll find in your travels. With 15 million people packed into just under 72,000 square miles, the region on paper might not suggest an abundance of wilderness, but as you'll see and probably already know, a rugged, character-shaping terrain waits in small patches and wide swaths all over this historic region. As it has been since before our country began, New England's landscape is defined by its glacial legacy, rolling monadnocks (isolated rocky mountains left standing tall when the glaciers eroded away the surrounding land), exposed granite ledges, kettle ponds (deep bodies of water created by chunks of melting glacier), and erratic boulders (dropped like giant breadcrumbs by glaciers in retreat). Unique rock formations and water features combine with one-of-a-kind plant and animal species and the local pride in observing nature through all four seasons to make hiking in New England a special experience for families.

This guide aims to provide kids of all ages a curated selection of some of the most varied and interesting destinations in New England while reassuring busy adults about what exactly to expect from any given trail, the features they will see when they arrive, and the logistics that can make or break an outdoor excursion with kids. I hope you get a sense of the love steeped in these pages—love for the outdoors, love for adventure, love for planning and preparation, and love for family and community. My family members were co-adventurers on every hike, tackling bathroom mishaps, downed trees, and even multiple hikes a day to test and compare, since choosing which adventures to include was no easy task. The number of kid-friendly hikes in New England is staggering, but I developed a firm Kid Filter, one that includes awesome features, simple driving and

< Rocky, rooty, flat, smooth, up, or down—no matter the trail, adventure beckons on the other side

turnkey instructions on the trail so you're not second-guessing yourselves, honest-to-goodness dirt on the bottom of your shoes rather than pavement, and no interpretive signs, all aimed at giving you a more adventurous and hike-like experience rather than a sterile stroll.

Many of us have seen the copious amounts of research about the benefits of getting kids outdoors more and interacting with the world in an open-ended way. As you romp with your own crew through the outdoors, just keep in mind that while the scavenger hunt items called out on each hike might help you to add excitement or teachable moments, finding them all should not be the main goal of your outing. I wrote this guide to help you get outside, spend time with your family, and have fun.

In 2006, smack in the middle of my second year of teaching fourth graders, I became a PolarTREC GoNorth! teacher explorer. I packed up with a top-notch, experienced adventure crew, and we set out to spend two weeks dog sledding, interviewing locals about climate change, and collecting snow-pack data. My number-one goal was to interpret the experience for my students back in my classroom and students from around the world who wanted to feel a piece of real-life adventure. Every night, our dogs rushed us through the snow to the next research hut in the middle of Finland. Once inside, we peeled off our layers, cooked dinner from our meal rations, used our maps to plan the next day, and got a good night's sleep. Then as now, I studied each day's route with the eyes of a child—finding the nooks that delighted me, asking myself big questions, documenting things that interested me but that I couldn't identify on the spot, and researching answers. A decade and a half later, I'm thrilled to be creating mini-adventures for New England families, helping them to become their own intrepid adventurers.

The driving question behind this book is how we can design experiences that inspire wonder in our children. That is the question to keep in mind as you use this book, too. If we can provide a fun environment and the initial sparks of curiosity, we can—as educators, caregivers, aunties and uncles, grandparents, and parents—help children discover and explore the world around them, creating a generation of resilient, curious kids who appreciate natural beauty even from the youngest of ages. This guide aims to give adults some tools to help ignite questions on the trail, to teach kids that it's great to stop and look at things instead of just rushing from point A to point B, and to begin to introduce a broader understanding of just how many unique places surround us in New England. By simply venturing out and interacting with kids along the trail, we are building the skills they need to learn how to question things they see around them—everywhere—and to look for answers.

Peter Gray, a Boston College research professor and expert on children's play, encourages parents to include other kids on adventures. "When you go on a hike or a trip, think about inviting other families or joining group hikes. Kids need other kids. This frees you, the adult, as well as your child, so you can interact with other adults. They can go ahead safely on the trail, and you don't have to go and amuse them because they are learning and playing with their peers. Don't try to cover too much ground—stop and let them play wherever they are."

< Nature's bounty offers
limitless creativity

Kids lead more structured lives today than ever before in history. I think you'll be pleasantly surprised when you see how much they enjoy simply being set loose in wide-open spaces. I hope this guide will help you foster curiosity and a love of nature in the kids in your life and that it helps to raise our next generation of naturalists by putting the guidebook in their hands. Many of the adventures in this book provide a taste of treks kids may embark on as college students or adults—imagine them tackling a list like the one at 4000footers.com. New England has a proud tradition of marking trail maps with red pen each time you complete a hike. I encourage you to grab your own pen and mark your achievements in guidebooks and maps as your family grows up. Experiencing the wonders all around us creates life-long habits of seeking out adventure, appreciating the gifts nature gives us every day, and caring about keeping our natural resources clean, beautiful, and accessible for future generations. All the scaffolds you'll need to plan even more of your own adventures are here.

CHOOSING YOUR ADVENTURE

This guide is designed to help children become co-adventurers with you across the diverse New England landscape, so build excitement by involving them in the planning process from the beginning. Let them flip through and mark the pages they'd like to tackle in the future. Ask them what features they love when they're outside. How hard do they feel like working today for their adventure? How long do they want to hike? The following tables can help you choose. For maximum success with younger kids, no hike is over 5 miles long or gains much more than 1,000 feet—perfectly attainable for most little legs. This means that there can be plenty of time for exploration, rest stops, snacks, and just taking in the sights and sounds around you.

ADVENTURES IN CONNECTICUT

ADVENTURE	NEAREST CITY	LENGTH (MILES)	DIFFICULTY & ELEVATION (FEET)	HIGHLIGHTS
1 **Great Ledge** PAGE 58	Danbury	1.5	Moderate 116'	Footbridges, views, toads, geology
2 **Leatherman Cave** PAGE 62	Hartford	1.6	Challenging 312'	History, cave
3 **Burr Pond** PAGE 66	Hartford	2.6	Moderate 99'	Pond, beach, boulders, history
4 **Mt. Tom Tower** PAGE 70	Litchfield	1.3	Moderate 336'	Tower, view, history, geology
5 **Campbell Falls** PAGE 74	Norfolk	1	Moderate 169'	Waterfall, geology, footbridges
6 **Meigs Point** PAGE 78	New Haven	1.1	Easy 7'	Bird-watching, seals, geology, beach
7 **Devil's Hopyard State Park** PAGE 82	Norwich	1	Moderate 67'	Cave, river, covered bridge, history
8 **Indian Chair at Mashamoquet Brook State Park** PAGE 86	Pomfret	2.8	Challenging 315'	Geology, cave, history

ADVENTURES IN RHODE ISLAND

ADVENTURE	NEAREST CITY	LENGTH (MILES)	DIFFICULTY & ELEVATION (FEET)	HIGHLIGHTS
9 Napatree Point Conservation Area PAGE 92	Westerly	3	Moderate 32'	Beach, ruins, history, bird-watching
10 Trustom Pond PAGE 96	Charlestown	2.5	Easy 33'	Bird-watching, boardwalk, ponds
11 Block Island National Wildlife Refuge PAGE 100	New Shoreham	1.2	Easy 32'	Bird-watching, beach, lighthouse, history
12 Fisherville Brook PAGE 104	Exeter	1.6	Easy 87'	History, bird-watching, pond, geology, footbridges
13 Stepstone Falls PAGE 108	Hopkinton	3.6	Moderate 123'	Waterfall, river, rock scrambling
14 Powder Mill Ledges PAGE 112	Greenville	1.2	Easy 76'	Bird-watching, pond, cool forest, boardwalks
15 Sachuest Point PAGE 116	Newport	2.6	Easy 29'	Beach, bird-watching, seals

ADVENTURES IN MASSACHUSETTS

ADVENTURE	NEAREST CITY	LENGTH (MILES)	DIFFICULTY & ELEVATION (FEET)	HIGHLIGHTS
16 **Cedar Tree Neck Sanctuary** PAGE 122	Vineyard Haven	1.4	Moderate 141'	Beach, pond, footbridges, boardwalks
17 **Fort Hill** PAGE 126	Eastham	1.6	Easy 51'	Beach, bird-watching, history, boardwalk
18 **World's End** PAGE 130	Hingham	3.1	Easy 92'	Geology, history, cool trees, boardwalk
19 **Ipswich River Wildlife Sanctuary** PAGE 134	Topsfield	1.5	Easy 79'	Bridges, bird-watching, rock grotto, pond
20 **Walden Pond** PAGE 138	Concord	1.7	Easy 49'	History, pond, beach
21 **Purgatory Chasm** PAGE 142	Worcester	0.7	Moderate 94'	Geology, deep canyon, rock scrambling
22 **Mt. Watatic** PAGE 146	Ashburnham	2.7	Challenging 588'	Summit, views, hawks, beaver pond, blueberries
23 **Doane's Falls** PAGE 150	Athol	1	Moderate 176'	Waterfalls, geology, bridge, history
24 **Goat Peak Tower at Mt. Tom** PAGE 154	Holyoke	1.2	Moderate 300'	Hawks, tower, views
25 **Peeskawso Peak** PAGE 158	Great Barrington	2.8	Challenging 664'	History, summit, views, cave
26 **Rounds Rock** PAGE 162	Lanesborough	0.7	Easy 110'	Views, airplane wreck, blueberries

ADVENTURES IN VERMONT

ADVENTURE	NEAREST CITY	LENGTH (MILES)	DIFFICULTY & ELEVATION (FEET)	HIGHLIGHTS
27 **Mt. Olga** *PAGE 168*	Wilmington	2	Moderate 521'	Tower, viewpoint, history
28 **Lye Brook Falls** *PAGE 172*	Manchester	4.6	Challenging 853'	Waterfall, geology, spring wildflowers, historic railroad
29 **Quechee Gorge** *PAGE 176*	Hartford	2	Easy 181'	Geology, bridge, waterfall, rock scrambling
30 **Wright's Mountain** *PAGE 180*	Bradford	1.8	Easy 453'	Cool cabin, viewpoint, geology, trail log
31 **Sunset Ledge** *PAGE 184*	Bristol	1.5	Moderate 343'	Rocky summit, views, the Long Trail
32 **Moss Glen Falls** *PAGE 188*	Stowe	0.5	Easy 100'	Waterfall, geology, footbridges

ADVENTURES IN
NEW HAMPSHIRE

ADVENTURE	NEAREST CITY	LENGTH (MILES)	DIFFICULTY & ELEVATION (FEET)	HIGHLIGHTS
33 Flume Gorge PAGE 194	Lincoln	1.9	Easy 469'	Waterfalls, geology, cave, boardwalks, bridge
34 Arethusa Falls PAGE 198	Hart's Location	2.8	Challenging 849'	Waterfalls, bridges, rock and root scrambling, river
35 Black Cap Mountain PAGE 202	Conway	2.3	Moderate 634'	Rocky summit, views, geology
36 White Lake PAGE 206	Tamworth	2	Easy 26'	Lake, beach, cool trees, bird-watching
37 West Rattlesnake Mountain PAGE 210	Holderness	1.9	Moderate 434'	Viewpoint, geology, bird-watching, lake
38 Mt. Major PAGE 214	Alton	2.8	Challenging 1,121'	Rocky summit, history, ruins
39 Blue Job Mountain PAGE 218	Farmington	2.2	Moderate 365'	Viewpoint, tower, rocky summit, blueberries, hawks
40 Pulpit Rock PAGE 222	Manchester	1.8	Moderate 102'	Footbridges, ravine, geology
41 Odiorne Point State Park PAGE 226	Portsmouth	2.1	Easy 16'	Jetty, history, ruins, marsh, beach

ADVENTURES IN MAINE

ADVENTURE	NEAREST CITY	LENGTH (MILES)	DIFFICULTY & ELEVATION (FEET)	HIGHLIGHTS
42 Bradbury Mountain PAGE 232	Freeport	1.2	Moderate 248'	Rocky summit, views, geology
43 Rattlesnake Pool PAGE 236	Fryeburg	2.1	Moderate 216'	Waterfalls, swimming, bridges, geology
44 Table Rock PAGE 240	Bethel	2.4	Challenging 939'	Rocky summit, iron ladders, viewpoint, Appalachian Trail
45 Moxie Falls PAGE 244	The Forks	2	Easy 226'	Waterfalls, boardwalks, geology
46 Debsconeag Ice Caves PAGE 248	Millinocket	2.4	Moderate 180'	Caves, ladder, rock scrambling, viewpoint
47 Little and Big Niagara Falls PAGE 252	Millinocket	2.4	Moderate 173'	Waterfalls, swimming, moose
48 Quoddy Head PAGE 256	Bangor	2.8	Easy 114'	Bog, historic lighthouse, whales, seashore, geology
49 Great Head PAGE 260	Bangor	1.4	Moderate 132'	Views, rock scrambling, beach, geology, ruins
50 Fernald's Neck Preserve PAGE 264	Camden	2.6	Moderate 115'	Bog, lake, geology, footbridges

∧ A young adventurer casts a line

ADVENTURES BY FEATURE

Can you remember the first cave you explored? The first waterfall that misted your face? Each of these adventures includes a destination or item of particular interest to motivate young legs and reward hard work. Encourage kids, as co-adventurers, to talk about which types of natural features tickle them the most and why.

FEATURE	ADVENTURE
Lakes	**3** Burr Pond **10** Trustom Pond **12** Upper Pond at Fisherville Brook **14** Powder Mill Ledges **16** Cedar Tree Neck Sanctuary **19** Ponds at Ipswich River Wildlife Sanctuary **20** Walden Pond **36** White Lake State Park **37** West Rattlesnake Mountain **50** Megunticook Lake at Fernald's Neck Preserve
Waterfalls	**5** Campbell Falls **13** Stepstone Falls **23** Doane's Falls **28** Lye Brook Falls **32** Moss Glen Falls **33** Flume Gorge **34** Arethusa Falls **43** Rattlesnake Flume and Pool **45** Moxie Falls **47** Little and Big Niagara Falls

FEATURE	ADVENTURE
History	**2** Leatherman Cave
	3 Dam at Burr Pond
	4 Mt. Tom Tower
	7 Covered bridge at Devil's Hopyard
	8 The wolf den at Indian Chair
	9 Fort Mansfield at Napatree Point
	11 Settlers' Rock and Cow Cove on Block Island
	12 Cemetery at Fisherville Brook
	17 Penniman House and Indian Rock at Fort Hill
	18 Carriage roads at World's End
	20 Thoreau's house site at Walden Pond
	25 Melville and Hawthorne's cave at Peeskawso Peak
	26 Plane wreck at Rounds Rock
	27 Fire tower at Mt. Olga
	28 Old railroad at Lye Brook Falls
	38 Hut at Mt. Major
	41 WWII remnants at Odiorne Point State Park
	48 Lighthouse at Quoddy Head
Flora and fauna	**6** Birds and seals at Meigs Point
	9 Bird-watching at Napatree Point
	10 Bird-watching and animal tracking at Trustom Pond
	12 Bird-watching at Fisherville Brook
	14 Bird-watching at Powder Mill Ledges
	17 Bird-watching at Fort Hill
	18 Bird-watching at World's End
	22 Blueberries, bird-watching, and beavers at Mt. Watatic
	26 Blueberries at Rounds Rock
	45 Spring wildflowers at Moxie Falls
	48 Bog and pitcher plants at Quoddy Head

FEATURE	ADVENTURE
Geology	**1** Granite at Great Ledge
	4 Glacial polish at Mt. Tom Tower
	5 Gneiss at Campbell Falls
	6 Glacial moraine at Meigs Point
	8 Indian Chair and Table Rock at Mashamoquet Brook State Park
	12 Glacial erratics at Fisherville Brook
	18 Drumlins at World's End
	21 Purgatory Chasm
	28 The Dalton Formation at Lye Brook Falls
	29 Quechee Gorge
	32 The Stowe Formation at Moss Glen Falls
	35 Glacial scratches at Black Cap
	37 Ledges at West Rattlesnake Mountain
	40 Pulpit Rock
	42 Granite at Bradbury Mountain
	43 Rattlesnake Pool and Flume
	49 Pink granite at Great Head in Acadia National Park
	50 Balancing Rock at Fernald's Neck Preserve
Caves	**2** Leatherman Cave
	7 Devil's Hopyard
	8 Wolf den at Mashamoquet Brook State Park
	25 Cave at Peeskawso Peak on Monument Mountain
	46 Debsconeag Ice Caves

FEATURE	ADVENTURE
Summits and views	**1** Great Ledge
	4 Mt. Tom Tower
	22 Mt. Watatic
	24 Goat Peak Tower on Mt. Tom
	25 Peeskawso Peak
	26 Rounds Rock
	27 Mt. Olga
	30 Wright's Mountain
	31 Sunset Ledge
	35 Black Cap
	37 West Rattlesnake Mountain
	38 Mt. Major
	39 Blue Job Mountain
	42 Bradbury State Park
	44 Table Rock
	46 Debsconeag Ice Caves
	49 Great Head
River and streams	**5** Whiting River at Campbell Falls
	7 Eightmile River at Devil's Hopyard State Park
	12 Fisherville Brook
	13 Falls River at Stepstone Falls
	23 Doane's Falls
	28 Lye Brook
	29 Ottauquechee River at Quechee Gorge
	32 Moss Glen Falls
	33 Pemigewasset River at Flume Gorge
	34 Bemis Brook at Arethusa Falls
	43 Rattlesnake Creek
	45 Moxie Falls
	47 Little Niagara Falls

FEATURE	ADVENTURE
Beach fun	**3** Burr Pond
	6 Meigs Point at Hammonasset State Beach
	9 Napatree Point
	11 Cow Cove at Block Island National Wildlife Refuge
	15 Sachuest Point
	16 Cedar Tree Neck Sanctuary
	17 Fort Hill
	20 Walden Pond
	36 White Lake State Park
	41 Odiorne Point State Park
	49 Sand Beach at Great Head
Campground by trailhead	**2** Black Rock State Park Campground by Leatherman Cave
	6 Hammonasset State Beach Park Campground at Meigs Point
	7 Devil's Hopyard State Park Campground
	8 Wolf Den Campground at Mashamoquet Brook State Park
	23 Tully Lake Campground near Doane's Falls
	26 Mt. Greylock Campground near Rounds Rock
	27 Molly Stark State Park Campground at Mt. Olga
	29 Quechee Gorge Campground
	30 Backpack to Wright's Mountain Cabin
	34 Dry River Campground at Arethusa Falls
	36 White Lake State Park Campground
	42 Bradbury Mountain State Park
	47 Daicey Pond Campground at Little and Big Niagara Falls
	49 Blackwoods Campground near Great Head

ADVENTURES BY SEASON

Many trails are available year-round for your adventuring pleasure, yet some really sing during particular moments of the year, so prepare your family to be ready for any season. Spring is often great for wildflower blooms or trails with waterfalls at maximum flow, but for some trails it's mud season—check conditions beforehand (and make sure the trail isn't closed), plan footwear, and consider a hiking stick or trekking poles. Summer allows the best access to more exposed, rocky trails that might be slippery or treacherous

∧ Fall is a favorite for many families in New England

during winter, along with special, higher-elevation wildflowers, but it also boasts copious flies and ticks—bring repellent and always do checks. In fall, many trails erupt with color and mushrooms, but some trails go near areas that allow hunting—always check the signs and consider bringing orange shirts and hats in your adventure bag. Winter can be a great time to escape crowds, especially if you bring your snowshoes or ice tracks. Keep in mind that any prime season (summer for hikes near swimming areas or fall for the most leafalicious hikes) means you might encounter crowds, so consider visiting early or late in the day, or try exploring during an "off-season." Allow your kids to understand the seasons by returning to a favorite hike throughout the year and asking them what's changed since their last visit.

PEAK SEASON	ADVENTURE	
Winter (snowshoes recommended)	12 Fisherville Brook 19 Ipswich River Wildlife Sanctuary	15 Sachuest Point 25 Peeskawso Peak 42 Bradbury Mountain
Spring	5 Campbell Falls 9 Napatree Point 10 Trustom Pond 12 Fisherville Brook	13 Stepstone Falls 15 Sachuest Point 23 Doane's Falls 28 Lye Brook Falls
Summer	3 Burr Pond 4 Mt. Tom Tower State Park 6 Meigs Point 16 Cedar Tree Neck Sanctuary 17 Fort Hill 20 Walden Pond 32 Moss Glen Falls 36 White Lake State Park	37 West Rattlesnake Mountain 39 Blue Job Mountain 41 Odiorne Point State Park 43 Rattlesnake Pool 45 Moxie Falls 46 Debsconeag Ice Caves 47 Little and Big Niagara Falls 48 Quoddy Head 49 Great Head
Fall	1 Great Ledge 2 Leatherman Cave 7 Devil's Hopyard 8 Indian Chair at Mashamoquet Brook State Park 11 Block Island National Wildlife Refuge 14 Powder Mill Ledges 18 World's End 21 Purgatory Chasm 22 Mt. Watatic 24 Goat Peak Tower 25 Peeskawso Peak	26 Rounds Rock 27 Mt. Olga 29 Quechee Gorge 30 Wright's Mountain 31 Sunset Ledge 33 Flume Gorge 35 Black Cap 38 Mount Major 40 Pulpit Rock 42 Bradbury Mountain 44 Table Rock 50 Fernald's Neck Preserve

PREPARING FOR YOUR ADVENTURE

This guide is a starter pack to a life full of adventure with your young ones. One day, your adventurers could be calling you up to ask if you want to summit Mount Washington with them. My own father took me out on hikes all over the country from toddlerhood, inspiring my thirst for outdoor adventure—flash forward a couple decades and he's coming with me on all of the hikes in this guide. One day, perhaps we'll tackle the Appalachian Trail, which powers its way 2181 miles from Springer Mountain, Georgia, to Mount Katahdin, Maine, and maybe your family will, too. In the meantime, work together to taste what each spectacularly diverse region has to offer and note which ones you want to return to in the future. The guide is organized as though you might be journeying along the Appalachian Trail itself—we'll start in Connecticut and work our way north to Maine.

INDIVIDUAL ADVENTURE PROFILES

Each of the fifty adventure profiles includes a basic trail map and information on the species of plants and wildlife, points of historic interest, and geological features that you may see on the trail. Allowing children to navigate using the maps and elevation guides, read the hike and species descriptions, and look for each featured item like a scavenger hunt puts the building blocks of adventure in their hands. Marking journeys on the map with points of interest gives relevance and context to kids' surroundings, so encourage them to note anything that stood out to them even if it's not noted in the book. You'll burst with pride when kids start to teach *you* what a lollipop loop is versus an out and back, are able to gauge whether they feel like just kickin' it on a hike with 200 feet of elevation gain or tackling 1000 feet, and make decisions about their own adventure. Each description is written for both you and the kids, so encourage them to read to themselves or out loud to you.

Elevation profile, length, type of trail, and time

An elevation profile is a line that sketches the general arch of the up and down during a hike. You'll notice a few are almost completely flat, and some are nearly a triangle. The elevation gain is how many feet you'll gain from start to finish; so even if it rolls up and then down again, if it says 300 feet that will be the total number of feet you'll have to walk up from the trailhead to the summit. No adventure is less than half a mile (too short to call a real excursion) or more than 5 miles (inaccessible for many of our younger or newer adventurers). The length of these hikes should give you plenty of time to enjoy the outing before anyone gets too tired. Embracing shorter trails translates into more time to savor them. Some of the routes

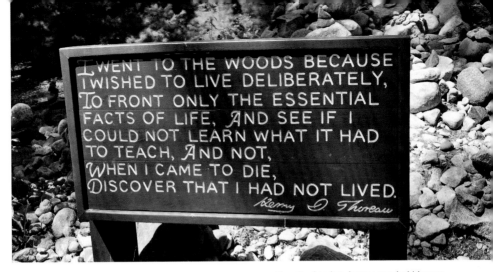

∧ New Englanders have a storied history of embracing the natural world

are shorter versions of a longer route and modified for kids—be sure to check out the land agency's map of whichever area you're visiting in case you want to explore more. Along with the length of the trail, I note whether the adventure is an out and back, a loop, or a lollipop loop and whether a clockwise or counterclockwise route is recommended.

An out and back has a clear final destination and turnaround point, and you'll cross back over what you've already discovered.

A loop provides brand-new territory the whole way around.

A lollipop is a straight line with a mini-loop at the end, like reaching a lake and then circling it, and heading back.

Talking with kids about the type of trail you're planning to hike will help young adventurers know what to expect. The estimated hike time includes time for exploration, and each adventurer's mileage may vary. Always give yourselves the delight of a relaxing hike with plenty of time to stop and play with a pile of fun-looking rocks, have leaf-boat races on a stream, or sketch a cool plant or animal.

Level of difficulty

This rating system was designed to facilitate a good time. It's important to note that these are kid-centric ratings; what's labeled as a "challenging" trail in this guide may not appear to be so challenging for a seasoned adult hiker. It can be fun to create your own rating for a trail when you're finished. "Did that feel like a level one, two, or three to you? Why?" Talking about it can help you understand your particular kid's adventure limits or help them seek new challenges. None of the trails in this book are paved (at least not all the way). Some are level and smooth, but due to New England's geological history, most have some combination of rocks and roots. There will be notes if a trail has exposed ledges or viewpoints where you'll want to hold smaller hands. Rocky terrain will cry for some sturdy shoes, and you'll want to have a bead on how wet, muddy, or snowy it may be to inform your decision of which pair will be best for your kid. It can help if you check reviews on AllTrails.com, Instagram, or websites like Mainehikers.com to get recent conditions and different families' opinions of the difficulty—you can also call the office of a nearby ranger station. While scouting these trails with my family, I saw many walking toddlers, strollers of every tire type imaginable, and baby backpacks on even the most challenging trails. I also spotted a couple sport strollers on moderately rocky trails with exposed roots. Use the information here to make informed decisions—every lead adventurer is different.

The adventures are rated as follows:

EASY These trails are typically short (1 mile or so), have low elevation gain, even, non-rocky terrain, and not too many exposed, hand-holding edges.

MODERATE These adventures have a bit more elevation gain (300 feet or so) and are likely to have a few hand-holding spots for the youngest hikers near exposed areas like cliffs or hillsides. The path itself may also be a bit rockier or rootier.

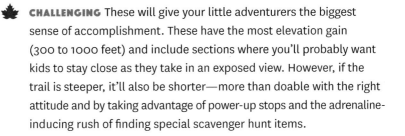 **CHALLENGING** These will give your little adventurers the biggest sense of accomplishment. These have the most elevation gain (300 to 1000 feet) and include sections where you'll probably want kids to stay close as they take in an exposed view. However, if the trail is steeper, it'll also be shorter—more than doable with the right attitude and by taking advantage of power-up stops and the adrenaline-inducing rush of finding special scavenger hunt items.

Season

This section lists the season when the adventure is possible; in many cases, trails can be hiked year-round. I also note the seasons when features of special interest can be seen, such as wildflowers or rushing waterfalls. Phenology is the study of how plants change across the seasons, and hikers are often the first to notice when leaves change colors or when a certain flower starts to bloom. Try taking the same hike in several seasons to teach your little adventurers about differences in the seasons, particularly for flora and fauna. The more often you go, the more likely you are to find something you may have missed the last time.

In winter and early spring, check with the local agency listed for each hike to make sure the trail and access road is actually open. In general, the higher up you go, the more likely you could be closed out by snow on either side of summer. Some adventures lend themselves to snow exploration without any gear, while others provide an opportunity to try snowshoes or ice tracks.

> *In Massachusetts (and the rest of New England too), we can do the same hike every week of the year and it might look completely different week to week.*
>
> —Aimee Tow, mom, Melrose, Massachusetts

Get there

When I was seven, my dad took our family out to the California desert in a small white Toyota pickup for our first off-roading experience. Our truck promptly got lodged between two rocks and towed out six hours later. Although that experience built some character and an adventurous spirit in me, I haven't included those kinds of roads in this guide. These adventures have all been road-tested at least once and specifically target trailheads with fairly easy access—meaning minimal dirt, gravel, or pothole-strewn roads. I'll leave those to our seasoned adventurers.

New England is big, folks. Almost 72,000 square miles. This guide is meant to be a sampling of diverse and beautiful areas all over the region. I hope that you and your children flip through and dream up road trips to the easternmost point of the United States, peering into the Atlantic from Quoddy Head State Park, or ferry rides to a blissfully quiet beach on Martha's Vineyard. Car time is a necessity to reach the amazing buffet of hikes available to you, New Englanders, and I hope you embrace the special family time that road trips can offer your crew.

Of course, you have your screen of choice, but consider a few fun ways to make the hours fly by fast, such as riddles, the A–Z game (you claim a point every time you see something that starts with the next letter of the alphabet), audiobooks, call-and-response type camp songs (ultimatecamp resource.com/site/camp-activities/camp-songs), nature journaling, and just good old-fashioned conversation. Always be ready to roll down windows for fresh air and encourage your little riders to look at the horizon if they start to get carsick. Oftentimes, I've sent you to a verified awesome spot in the midst of *even more to explore*. I encourage you to always stop by visitor centers, make the most of every trip, and consider finding somewhere nearby to camp to enjoy the area for longer.

Basic longhand directions to the trailhead are listed with each adventure, along with a *case-sensitive* link to Google Maps you can drop directly into your smartphone browser. Be sure to do this before you head out, while you are certain to have coverage. You can also get free highway maps

∧ Maine's open roads
beckon in fall

mailed to you or printed, which can be helpful and educational for your little co-pilot (check the tourism website for each state, such as visitnh.gov/contact-us). Before leaving home, you and your adventurer can geek out on Google Earth or turn on satellite view in Google Maps to walk your route (and sometimes even trail) step by step.

There's something magical about maps, and each map in this guide was carefully designed with kids in mind to be touched, traced, and held out in front of them to understand their surroundings. Encourage your kids to understand the difference between roads, highways, and interstate freeways. We've simplified the maps so kids can focus on the land agencies they'll be visiting, the closest towns with grub stops, and the larger adventure hub cities nearby. Hopefully, while they adventure with you, they'll start to build a sixth sense for using maps. Ask them navigation questions. How long will this adventure take, do you think? Where does that river start, and how is it related to the ocean? How many turns will we need to make? What's our next highway? Any cities nearby? Any fun names you can see? Just asking questions can encourage curiosity and leadership in your young adventurers.

Restrooms

We can't have a hiking book for kids without chatting about bathrooms. Many trails have pit toilets or developed toilets right at the parking lot. If not, plan on a restroom stop in the nearest town or gas station on your way in and on your way out. Discuss appropriate trail bathroom etiquette with your kids as well, such as heading safely off the trail, away from water, and properly covering it should the need arise. Pack your adventure bag with what you need to be comfortable, such as a Ziploc bag with toilet paper. Don't leave any toilet paper behind to spoil someone else's experience; make sure to pack it back out.

Parking and fees

Your main goal, lead adventurers, is to get out on the trail. If thinking about how to park and pay gets your boot laces knotted up, rest assured that as long as you have some cash in the glove compartment, the team will be just fine. All the trailheads listed here have a parking lot or pullout and some sort of trail sign indicating where you are and whether you need a parking pass or permit. For some, you'll need to plan ahead and get a day pass or annual pass before you get to the trailhead. Others have self-service pay stations at the trailhead—either those accepting credit cards or an "iron ranger" with a slot in it for a fee envelope with cash or check—and you'll affix the pass to your car. Many parking lots are free, though, and each is noted. Many are free for in-state residents but have a fee for out-of-state visitors (residency is usually determined by your car's license plate). There are several "fee-free days," including National Public Lands Day in September and many holidays.

∧ A roadside pie dispensary is just one example of the many grub stops you'll drive by on each adventure

Treat yourself

To reward yourselves, the guide lists nearby cafes and restaurants for good, quick bites, in part so you can plan whether you need to pack substantial snacks or just a few with you on the trail. These are road-tested yummy bakeries, ice cream shops, burger joints, and family-friendly diners with notable items or spaces that your kids will enjoy. Regional treats like maple creemees, cider and cider donuts, whoopie pies, popovers, lobster rolls, and chowder beckon after many hikes.

Managing agencies

I've listed the name of the agency that manages each hiking trail, along with its telephone number and pertinent social media handles. Before heading out, it's a good idea to check on current conditions, including weather, roads, wildlife sightings, and any hazards that haven't been cleared or fixed. The folks on the other end are often rangers and are generally thrilled to share information about their trails. They can also connect you to botanists, geologists, historians, and other experts. I received fast and enthusiastic responses from many of the rangers behind the Facebook pages of these parks—involve your kids and encourage them to say hello and ask about conditions or an unanswered question from the trail.

Following the trail

In New England, colorful blazes on trees and rocks mark the way along most trails. While we have made every effort to pick straightforward trails that are hard to get lost on, it's good to build the habit of always looking for the next blaze and question your path if you haven't seen one in a while. In our family, it's a coveted prize to be the first person to see each blaze. Another good habit to encourage in your kids is taking a moment at each

power-up stop to note the landmarks around them and check to see what comes next on the map. These skills will help them out when they get older and graduate from this guide to more difficult trails. Give a hug to a tree with a blaze on it and send a mental thank you to the land agencies that maintain the blazes and make outdoor adventure possible for us all.

< Blazes mark the way on most trails in this guide

Scavenger hunts

The scavenger hunt included with each adventure invites you to look for specific fungi, plants, animals, minerals, and historical items of interest. You'll find descriptions and photos of trees, leaves, flowers, seeds, cones, bark, nuts, wildlife or animal tracks, fur and feathers, rocks and geological features, historically significant landmarks or artifacts, natural features such as lakes, rivers, and waterfalls, or culturally significant spots that appear on each trail. Entries have questions to ponder or activities to try, and, when applicable, you can dig into the scientific genus and species and learn why a plant or animal is called what it is. Encourage kids to "preview" what they might see on the trail, and if they think they've found it, take out the book to match. Take it up a notch and encourage them to make their *own* scavenger hunt—write down five things they think they might see on the trail today, from very basic (at least five trees) to very specific (five eastern white pine cones on the ground).

IDENTIFYING WHAT YOU FIND

Eighty percent of New England is covered by forest and it's full of plants, fungi, mammals, invertebrates, reptiles, and amphibians. Identifying these species in the wild involves using clues from size, leaves, bark, flowers, and habitat. Work with kids to ask questions that will move them from general identification (Is it a conifer or evergreen or a deciduous tree?) to the specifics (What shape are the leaves? What species is this?). The species of trees, shrubs, mushrooms, wildflowers, and animals listed in the scavenger hunts were chosen because you should be able to find them with ease and because there's something interesting about them that might appeal to children. You may not find every species on the trail every time, however. It's best to adopt the attitude of considering it a win when you do find one, and to present those you can't find as something to look forward to for next time.

Tristan Gooley, author of *The Natural Navigator*, encourages kids to look for "keys" as they walk on trails. "Keys are small families of clues and signs. If we focus on them repeatedly, they can give us a sixth sense." Start noticing which way the sun is when you start and when you end, and where the natural features (hills, mountains) are around you. Use a compass (there's probably one on your smartphone) to start understanding direction and building this natural sixth sense Gooley speaks of.

*For observing changes in a forest, the key is to keep an eye out for changes in composition, such as a hardwood forest becoming a conifer forest, and changes in structure, such as a forest with small, dense trees becoming one with larger, more widely spaced trees. This can help you start to see patterns instead of just a continuous forest blur. Use inquiry and ask questions—**parents don't need to have the answers**. The questions themselves are way more important because they cause kids to look more closely at things and come up with ideas to try to explain them. I take my students to two forests that have visible differences, such as a lumpy forest floor versus one that's smooth, and have them try to figure out why.*

—Tom Wessells, terrestrial ecologist and author of *New England's Roadside Ecology*

When you find a particularly interesting species that's not mentioned in the scavenger hunt, have kids either sketch it or take a photo of it. Remind them to look it up later, either in a printed field guide to the region or on a specialty website such as wildflowersearch.com or iNaturalist.org. Including basic descriptions and the name of the region in your search will help kids find their treasure in online field guides. LeafSnap.com and the Seek app by iNaturalist are also great for creating species treasure hunts on the trail.

Look at the things you encounter from different scales and different angles and different parts. Say a tree—you have a really large organism and you might need to stand really far away to see a picture of it. But look closer—and find the fruit on the ground, look at the bark, look at the leaves. Think of all of the different characteristics that can help you learn what it is, why it lives where it is. Start recognizing all of the pieces of an organism, and thinking how to capture those photographically if you want to share that record with the world. Try to find the part of the thing that is most unique-looking and try to fill the frame with that with a nice, clear photo.

—Carrie Seltzer, iNaturalist

If you're ready to level up everyone's identification skills, join the Native Plant Trust, the Northeast Mycological Federation (for mushrooms), or the botanical or native plant society for your state. All have great Facebook groups, newsletters, or online forums where you can share

photos of a species you can't identify or confirm that a certain species is growing or blooming where you hiked. The USA National Phenology Network (usanpn.org) allows kids to contribute to science by entering their observations of seasonal changes into a nationwide database, and it has a cool Junior Phenologist Program and kid-friendly resources to boot. Joining your local chapter of societies and organizations also means getting invited to their fun, themed group hikes on topics such

< So many treasures to find on the trail

as wildflowers, fungi, and everything in between. Plus, you're exposing your kids to the power of a community resource where everyone is passionate about nature and science and wants to help one another.

David Yih of the Connecticut Botanical Society suggests starting your plant ID journey with trees. "Trees are a great place to start, as there are fewer to keep straight and because some have interesting tastes and smells that are fun to experience. Scrape off the bark of a twig with your fingernail and see if it has a pleasant fragrance like black birch (*Betula lenta*) does—it can help you identify the tree. Observe leaf arrangement along the stalk of a plant or the branch of a tree. Do the leaves grow in opposite pairs, do they alternate, or do they form groups of more than two at the same spot (whorled)? Those are important distinctions to make when learning to identify plants. For example, fewer kinds of trees have opposite leaves, so that narrows it down."

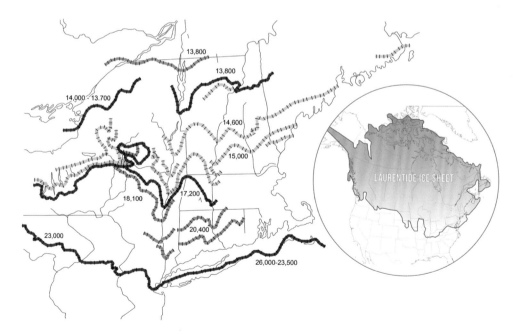

New England's geography and geology were very much shaped by glaciers. Twenty-three thousand years ago a glacier called the Laurentide Ice Sheet had reached south from Canada to cover all of New England—it was several miles thick on top of the land you'll explore—but by around 12,000 years ago the glaciers had retreated, leaving behind a unique landscape. It's a really cool place to explore rocks and geology. When you encounter interesting rock colors, folds, and structures, encourage children to think about the rock cycle—a rock's evolution from igneous to metamorphic to sedimentary—and how rocks build up in formations over time. Use the scavenger hunts to build a familiarity with New England's granites and glacial erratic boulders so your kids can start to find them and notice the subtle differences. Ask questions—what does the texture of the rock look like? What color is it? Does it feel heavy or light? Is it hard or soft? Does it break easily? Join a regional geological society—each state has one: Connecticut (geologicalsocietyct.org), Rhode Island (web.uri.edu/geo/rhode-island-geological-survey), Massachusetts (massgeosociety.org), Vermont (uvm.org/vtgeologicalsociety), New Hampshire (gsnh.org), and Maine (gsmmaine .org)—for newsletters, group hikes, and community opportunities. You can even join the National Speleological Society if you're interested in caves.

< Check out how the Laurentide Ice Sheet slowly receded over time, leaving behind all the great boulders you'll explore. These lines show how many thousands of years ago it melted as it receded—you'll follow the remnants of this glacier throughout your adventures.

< How is this 1685 map of New England different from today's map? How might the map look different in the future?

Historical items

Join your local historical society to start to identify items of historical interest on New England's trails. Each state, sometimes even a specific region of a state, has its own historical society with resources and an email and phone number to ask questions: Connecticut (chs.org), Rhode Island (rihs.org), Massachusetts (masshist.org), Vermont (vermonthistory.org), New Hampshire (nhhistory.org), and Maine (mainehistory.org). Parents can foster inquiry with each hike.

Gregg Mangan from Connecticut Humanities enthuses, "The great thing about inquiry and history is that it doesn't involve memorizing facts and dates but exploring larger questions about why things are and how they got that way. It is so easy to pass by a statue or structure in your town every day and never think about how it got there, what purpose it served, or the larger story behind it. Rather than reading about history in textbooks, inquiry encourages teachers, parents, and students to engage with their communities, ask questions, and go find the answers to these questions by locating and reviewing the primary sources (documents, diaries, photographs) themselves. In this way, they learn research skills, how to evaluate evidence, and how to form their own conclusions rather than reading someone else's."

POWER-UP STOPS

Liz Thomas has hiked over 20,000 miles and is a former speed record holder for the Appalachian Trail. Her biggest tip for young adventurers learning to build stamina is, "Understand your body. Kids are just figuring out to read their bodies. You can think of your body as having gauges and you're the pilot at the front of the plane. Your goal is to keep your gauges (hydration, exposure, food) in the happy zone." She even sets reminders on her watch to drink and eat as she walks from sunrise to sunset. As lead adventurers, you'll be keeping a close eye on these gauges but also helping kids recognize them, anticipate them, and power through them.

For each adventure, I note key places that serve as mini-milestones or power-up stops. Be sure to pack snacks for kids to eat at these stops to keep blood sugar, energy levels, and mood high. Remember that this amount of physical activity may be challenging for little ones. Often, these power-up stops are at points of interest: fun bridges, switchbacks before a small hill, or overlooking a viewpoint. Stopping for a moment can fuel you up, give you a chance to listen to the wind or animals around you, watch what's going on in the woods, and prepare you for the larger goal of finishing the adventure itself.

Power-ups can also be great for a nursing mom or bottle-feeding dad or for tending to other little ones' needs, as well as for question-based games like "I Spy." As the lead adventurer, use these stops for inspiration, play, questions, games, and riddles, and encourage your kids to do the same. Don't underestimate the power of choosing a special snack to serve as a particular motivator on tough ascents or rainy days.

Bridges make great places to relax and explore >

∧ A family sets out prepared
to climb Mt. Tom Tower

ADVENTURE BAG, SUPPLIES, AND SAFETY

Start your kids on a lifelong habit of packing an adventure bag, whether it's the smallest satchel or the largest consumer-grade backpack they can actually hold. The art of having everything you need with you without being too burdened is key to having a good time on the trail. All of these adventures are short enough that even if you did pack too much, its weight won't jeopardize your enjoyment levels too heavily.

NAVIGATION In addition to the maps in this book, consider investing in a compass and full trail map of the area (Appalachian Mountain Club maps are the gold standard). Make sure your smartphone is fully charged, with offline maps available and the compass feature handy. My family likes to carry an extra portable battery for our phones.

"Our kids would learn the weather report and typical conditions prior to an adventure and stage a gear list. Then they'd organize their gear by what they would wear and what they needed to pack. Same for food, hydration, and miscellaneous gear. After packing they'd line up their gear for an inspection or 'shakedown.' We'd perform similar exercises for route planning and use teachable moments while on an adventure to discuss how our planning and preparation resulted. Did it rain and did we have our rain gear? Was it chilly in exposure and did we have our beanie? Did we have enough food and hydration? The kids really enjoyed the planning and execution and we liked the fact they were involved in the process. The best part is the lessons learned indirectly applied to their day-to-day lives and we definitely saw positive impacts on how they managed other responsibilities."

—Stephen Bailey, father of Zachary and Denali from Windham, Maine

 HYDRATION Bring plenty of water for everyone and remember to drink along the way.

 NUTRITION Consider the length of the trail and the amount and type of snacks you'll need to keep the train going.

 FIRE Pack a lighter or matchbook for emergencies.

 FIRST AID KIT This can range from a mini–first aid kit with essentials such as bandages and aspirin to much heftier options with space blankets. Consider what you want your car stocked with and what you want on the trail with you.

 TOOLS A small knife or multi-tool goes a long way in the woods.

ILLUMINATION Did you explore just a wee bit too long and dusk is approaching? A simple headlamp, flashlight, or even your phone's flashlight can help lead the way.

SUN AND INSECT PROTECTION If it's an exposed trail, consider sunglasses, sunscreen, and hats for you and the kids. When the weather is warm many trails have mosquitoes, flies, and ticks, so be prepared with your favorite method of repelling them.

SHELTER You may want a space blanket or small tarp in your adventure bag in case of emergency.

INSULATION Check the weather together and decide the type of protection and warmth you want to bring. A second layer is always a good idea—breezes can chill even the warmest of days, and New England weather is famously hard to predict, especially in the mountains.

Fun items to have on hand might include a nature journal and pen or pencil, hand lens, binoculars, a bug jar for capturing and releasing spiders and insects, a camera, a super-special treat for when you reach the top of something, a container for a special mushroom or pine cone, and even a favorite figurine or toy that your littles are currently enamored with so they interact with that tree stump up ahead. Wet wipes, toilet paper, and Ziploc bags are also recommended. First-timer? Join the local chapter of a hiking group like Hike it Baby or the Appalachian Mountain Club to hike with your peers and learn the ropes of packing.

While it may be handy for you to navigate to trailheads using your smartphone, remember that many wilderness areas have spotty cell service. As a general safety practice for hiking with kids, always tell a third party where you are going and when you expect to be back, and remember to tell anyone who may need to get ahold of you that you're not certain of cell coverage in the area. If you adventure a lot, you might want to consider an affordable satellite GPS, like those made by Garmin, that allows you to send texts from areas that don't have cell service. On the trail itself, every lead adventurer will have his or her own comfort level with safety, and you'll determine when your children will need hand-holding or reminders to stay close as you get near tricky terrain, exposed edges, or water.

Mark Twain once said, "One of the brightest gems in the New England weather is the dazzling uncertainty of it. There is only one thing certain about it, you are certain there is going to be plenty of weather." Teaching awareness and common sense and fostering an attitude of "there's no bad weather, only the wrong clothing" in these situations will go a long way toward creating an adventurous and resilient child. You can model this "love the unlovable" attitude by remaining upbeat and playful as lead adventurer, and you'll be amazed at how quickly their attention will turn back to the trail and its wonders.

Lenore Skenazy, president of Let Grow (a nonprofit promoting independence as a critical part of childhood) and founder of the Free-Range Kids Movement, understands you might be nervous about shepherding your family into the unknown. "I'm often asked, 'What if something goes wrong?' I love to ask back, 'Can you remember something that went wrong when you were a kid, playing with other kids?' People often look back so fondly on that time when things went wrong. There's even a word for the way we treasure imperfect things and moments: *wabi-sabi*, from the Japanese practice of filling a crack in a vase with gold, because the imperfection is what makes it beautiful. The outdoors is never without some surprises and even minor risks, but neither is the indoors. My guess is all adults can remember when something went wrong and it's a treasured (if only in retrospect) memory. Imperfection is inevitable and valuable. Embrace it!"

In addition to weather, poison ivy is a common hazard lurking in New England's woods, but once you can identify it, you'll be able to spot it with almost infrared vision. Touching this plant causes a blistering rash in most people. Remember the warning "Leaves of three, let it be"—though the plant can grow as a spreading vine or a low or upright shrub, its groups of three

< Poison ivy (*Toxicodendron radicans*)

leaflets make it easy to identify. New leaves start out red, then fade to a yellowy bronze before turning fully green in summer and bright red, orange, or yellow in late summer and fall.

Aside from moose and deer on the road, New England doesn't have much in the way of large dangerous animals. Eastern black bears (*Ursus americanus*), coyotes (*Canis latrans*), and bobcats (*Lynx rufus*) are shy of humans, and you're quite unlikely to encounter them on hikes. If it is a possibility, trailheads will often have information on animals in the area and reminders of how to take precautions. By helping kids be aware on the trail, looking for signs of wildlife and understanding what to do during an encounter, you can create a lifelong safety skillset for adventuring. Please also be aware of all trailhead signs; if hunting is permitted in fall and winter, you'll want to wear bright orange on your head and body—we'll call out specific trails where this applies, but it's always good to research this ahead of time for your destination.

The most dangerous critter in New England is arguably *Ixodes scapularis*, the deer tick or blacklegged tick, which can spread Lyme disease. Knowledge of ticks, tick-borne diseases, and tick prevention and safety is essential and goes hand in hand with hiking. Ticks don't fly or jump; they attach to animals that come into direct contact with them, then they feed on the blood (yours, your dog's, other

∧ Ticks are small. Be sure to check for them carefully.

mammals). They love shrubby, grassy areas—be sure to stick to the center of the trail and don't go off-trail. Before a hike, consider wearing light clothing so you can quickly spot any ticks that have hitched a ride. Consider treating your clothes with 0.5 percent permethrin or 20–30 percent DEET (be sure to apply for your children, avoiding eyes, nose, and mouth). Make full-body tick checks a part of your hiking routine when you get back to the car. Be sure to check under your arms, behind your knees and ears, and between your toes. Shower or bath time at home provides another chance for a full-body check. If you find a tick, remove it with tweezers as close to your skin as possible, don't handle it with your bare hands, clean the area with soap and water, and call your doctor. Ticks can be found in almost any season so it's best to always perform checks.

NATURE JOURNALING

I received my first nature journal in Sydney, Australia, on my first night as a National Geographic Fellow with a group of students and teachers from around the world. It was leather-bound and bursting with empty pages just begging to be doodled and documented on (I now have six and counting). Catherine Hughes, retired head of the *National Geographic Kids* magazine education team, gently guided us with a few key maxims for nature journaling:

 Make quick, messy field notes. You can add details later when you have free time, like on the drive home. You don't have to be a great artist to sketch something you see.

 Sketch the map of the adventure that day.

 Personalize it. Did someone say something funny? What was the most unique thing that happened on the adventure?

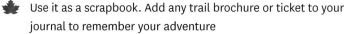 Use it as a scrapbook. Add any trail brochure or ticket to your journal to remember your adventure

A great trail is a story—it has a beginning, a true climax or crux, and then an end, whether back the way you came or wrapping up in a loop. As you review your outings with young adventurers, encourage them to feel the story of the trail. How did they like the beginning? What was the climax? How did it end? What characters (plants, rock formations, or animals) stood out to them? A fun after-hike activity is taking your nature journal and writing a fictional account of what happened on the trail, making the landscape come alive in a whole new way.

Consider picking out a small blank journal for kids to bring along in their adventure bags. When you stop for lunch at your destination, at power-up stops, on the ride home, or later that night, encourage your little adventurers to create drawings of things they saw, document their observations of trees or animals, or press leaves or flowers.

Jaedon sketches the tracks of a seagull in the sand

DIGITAL CONNECTIONS

The social media accounts of many of the agencies that manage public lands in New England are quite active, and they can be a great way for kids to use technology to enhance their experience in nature. Together, you can ask pre- or post-adventure questions about conditions or flora and fauna, and the forums can be wonderful vehicles for sharing images you snapped— for both you and your little adventurer. Search the location on Instagram for recent photos and be sure to geo-tag yours to contribute to other hikers' searches as well. Enhance the journey and encourage kids to define what stood out to them about the experience with a coauthored trip report on one of these sites:

 Local options like MaineTrailFinder.com Dive deep into specific states—kids can help out the community by adding photos and comments after they hike.

AllTrails.com This a crowd-sourced database of hikes built by a community of 4 million registered members that includes reviews, user-uploaded photos, and downloadable maps. Meaghan Praznik, head of communications at AllTrails, says, "We all know *why* the outdoors are important. Health benefits, physical benefits, and what it does for us mentally. At the end of the day, we want AllTrails to be the *how*. We want features that will take away stress on how to get outside, because the outdoors should be your escape from the stress. From sorting based on the area you're in, to providing driving directions to the trailhead to filtering based on criteria suitable for you, whether that's for a new hike going out alone with three kids or something dog-friendly, we want to make sure we're giving people the confidence to hit the trail."

🍁 **wildflowersearch.com** This site has many good tools for identifying flowers. It's as simple to use as uploading a photo and asking it to scan a database for you. It also has up-to-date lists of species in bloom.

🍁 **iNaturalist.org and Seek by iNaturalist** This web- and app-based online community allows you to share your species observations with other naturalists around the world. It's also a great place to post a question if you can't identify something you found.

🍁 **Geocaching.com or the Geocaching app** Geocaches are treasures hidden by other people with GPS coordinates posted online. If you're heading out on one of the adventures, check the website or app to see if anyone has hidden a treasure along the trail. If they have, you can use your phone to navigate to it, find it, exchange a treasure item or sign the log, and hide it back where you found it. About twelve years ago I hid one on a trail, and it's been found more than 500 times!

SMARTPHONES

You may have picked up this book to find ways of distracting kids from their phones. Not using a phone at all during your adventures can be fun and appropriate, and you probably already know where you stand on the issue of screen time, but if you want to try a balance, letting kids use their phone on the trail to take a picture of an interesting flower, navigate with a digital compass app, use the audio app to capture a birdsong, or share their pictures of the hike on the state forest's Instagram can be a conscientious way to bridge technology and outdoor time (just be sure the phone is put away more than it is out).

∧ Kids love using phone cameras to capture scenic views—let them be the official photographer on your hikes

SHOWING RESPECT FOR NATURE

New England has 15 million lovely people, and enjoying and protecting its land will be key to conserving its beauty for generations to come. We are inspiring stewards—the more we are out there understanding and delighting in the natural world with our families, the more we and our little adventurers want to take care of it in the future. Some of the beautiful areas in this guide are also the most remote and precious. You're doing the most important thing you can to keep the region beautiful—taking your kids outside.

You can't help but feel a part of something larger when you and your kids get yourselves on top of a fire tower overlooking fall colors or squeeze through a glacial chasm formed thousands of years ago. By simply noticing and beginning to identify features, flora, and fauna in nature you're creating a sense of respect and appreciation. Model and embrace the "Leave No Trace" ethos (see LNT.org for more great ideas) on each and every trail. Be diligent with snack wrappers and the flotsam and jetsam of your adventure bag. Be sure to always stay on the trail and avoid trampling vegetation and disturbing wildlife to ensure that everyone and everything can share the adventure.

The scavenger hunts will be asking kids to act as young naturalists, to notice, touch, and play with nature around them in a safe and gentle way. For the most part, try not to take a leaf or flower off a growing plant, but rather collect and play with items that are already on the ground. Manipulate them, stack them, create art with them, trace them in journals—but then leave them to be used by the other creatures on the trail, from the fungi decomposing a leaf to another kid walking down the trail tomorrow. Many of these wilderness areas and public lands were created with leaders in New England, and you're creating the next generation of conservationists simply by getting kids out in them.

ADVENTURES IN
CONNECTICUT

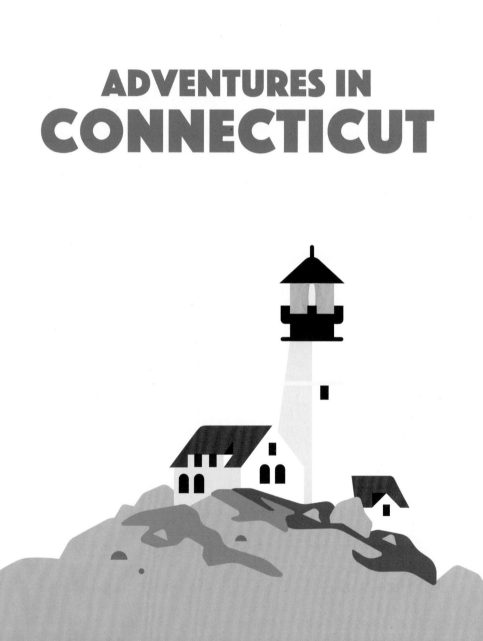

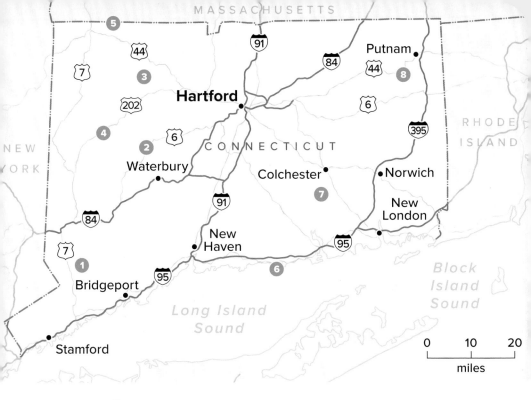

Adventurers, let's begin in the southwest of the Nutmeg and Constitution State and work our way up. The name Connecticut comes from the word *Quinnehtukqut* in the Algonquian language, meaning "the long river." It refers to the Connecticut River, New England's longest at 406 miles, which flows southward right through the middle of the state. You'll explore the northern border of the Long Island Sound, a valley formed around 200 million years ago by volcanic eruptions, Mattatuck State Forest, the Taconic Mountains in the Appalachian Range, and the slopes of Mount Frissell, which boasts the highest point in the state at 2380 feet. Despite the trees that cover the land now, you can still see the effects of the ice sheet that covered Connecticut thousands of years ago. You'll stop at the Great Ledge, follow an old vagabond's route to his cave hideout, circle a pond, take in the view from a tower, visit waterfalls, and find a wolf's den. Take in the state motto—"He who transplanted still sustains"—and transplant and sustain yourselves on as many trails as you can.

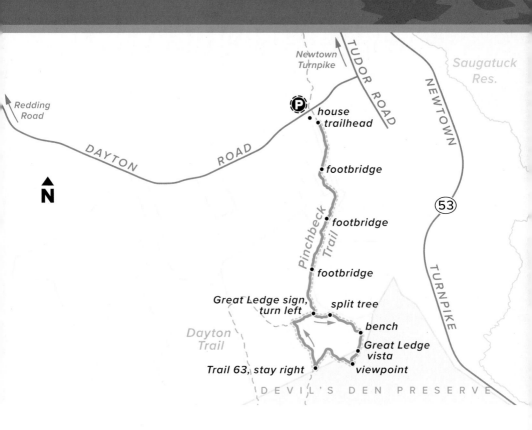

GAZE OVER THE GREAT LEDGE

YOUR ADVENTURE

Adventurers, you're following the white blazes of the Pinchbeck Trail to the Great Ledge Loop on the historic homelands of the Paugussett and Poquonnuc, managed today by the Nature Conservancy and Redding Land Trust. After walking half a mile through the dense, ferny forest and crossing over three fun footbridges, you'll find the Great Ledge sign. Take a left here for your lollipop loop—you'll get peeks through the trees at the view as you get

Elevation Gain 116ft.

ELEV [FT]

600–

350–

DISTANCE [MI]

LENGTH **1.5-mile** lollipop loop

HIKE + EXPLORE 1 hour

DIFFICULTY Moderate—short, not much exposure except for hand-holding for littles by the ledges

SEASON Year-round. Fall has great foliage; mid-June has mountain laurel and other blooms.

GET THERE From Danbury, head south on CT-53. Turn right on Tudor Road at Saugatuck Reservoir, then right on Dayton Road after half a mile. The parking lot is on your right. After parking, cross Dayton Road and walk up a small paved road beside a house to the trailhead on your left.

Google Maps: bit.ly/timbergreatledge

RESTROOMS None

FEE None

TREAT YOURSELF Heibeck's Stand claims to have the best hot dog in the state—drive just 10 minutes east to decide for yourself.

Redding Land Trust, The Nature Conservancy
(203) 568-6270
Instagram @Nature_Connecticut | Facebook @ReddingLandTrust @CT.NatureConservancy

∧ Stand on the Great Ledge for expansive views of Saugatuck Reservoir

closer. The granite ledges are perfect for a power-up stop, but be cautious near the edges. Check out the 12-*billion*-gallon Saugatuck Reservoir below, which provides water for surrounding towns—be sure to say thank you to it as you take a big gulp from your water bottle. Picnic on a log bench or find a flat spot on the ledge and contemplate how the citizens of nearby Redding advocated to preserve this land so adventurers like you could enjoy it forever. Do you have a favorite piece of land in your town you would like to preserve for everyone? After taking in several viewpoints, pass Trail 63, staying to the right, and find your way back to the Pinchbeck Trail you started on. Continue back to the trailhead.

SCAVENGER HUNT

American toad
Keep a keen eye on the ground for this common toad. They like shady spots and are often nocturnal, which means active at night. Stop and observe one for a few minutes—you might see it eating one of the one thousand insects it can devour in a single day. Listen for its long, high-pitched call (bit.ly/timbertoad). Can you make a noise like that?

< *Anaxyrus americanus* rests underneath the foliage

Bolete mushroom
Keep your eyes peeled for fungi on the ground. This kind is a bolete, and it's different than a gilled mushroom. Get low on the ground and peek under its cap—boletes have pores (small round holes) instead of gills.

A reddish bolete mushroom pokes up from the dirt >

Jewelweed

Look for jewelweed's ovate (round like an egg) leaves with soft teeth on the edge and, during summer and fall, a bright orange flower with red spots. Rain or dew will sometimes bead up on its petals and look like little jewels. It's also called touch-me-not, because of its hanging seedpods that form in fall—the slightest touch triggers a spring inside the pod to burst open and spread the seeds.

< *Impatiens capensis* blooms in late summer and early fall

Eastern white pine

Look for the five needles of this conifer (a tree that makes cones). It loves to dig its roots in the cracks of ledges. Feel its bark and imagine using its trunk for a ship mast, like early colonists did. Find some bark on the ground to construct your own mini-ship.

Pinus strobus needles grow in bundles of five >

Interrupted fern

Many kinds of fern carpet this hike. Can you recognize their differences? This fern has a stalk with rounded pinnae (a kind of leaf) on opposite sides. In fall, the fronds turn bright yellow. In winter, they turn brown and die, but in spring, new leaves grow and the process begins all over again, making this a deciduous plant. What is something you start over every year?

< *Osmunda claytoniana* stands out in the crowd with its rounded pinnae

2

LOUNGE AT LEATHERMAN CAVE

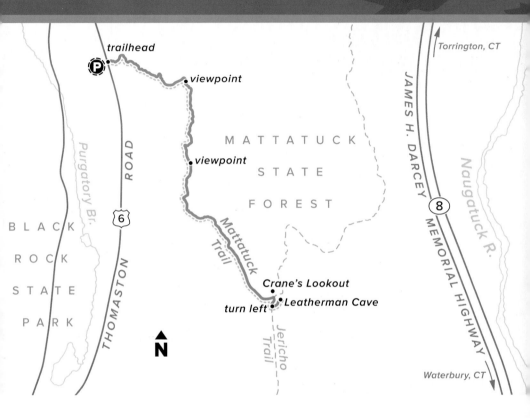

trailhead

viewpoint

MATTATUCK

STATE

FOREST

Purgatory Br.

ROAD

6

THOMASTON

viewpoint

Mattatuck Trail

Crane's Lookout

turn left • Leatherman Cave

Jericho Trail

N

BLACK

ROCK

STATE

PARK

JAMES H. DARCEY

Torrington, CT

Naugatuck R.

8

MEMORIAL HIGHWAY

Waterbury, CT

YOUR ADVENTURE

Adventurers, you're walking in the footsteps of the Leatherman, who became famous in the nineteenth century for tramping the same circuit, over and over, for more than three decades while wearing a handmade suit of stitched leather scraps that weighed 60 pounds. How heavy are your clothes today? You'll begin at the pullout on Highway 6 and follow the

ELEV [FT]
850–
350–
Elevation Gain
312ft.
DISTANCE [MI]
1   2   3   4

∧ Wind your way through this historic cave

LENGTH

1.6 miles out and back

HIKE + EXPLORE 2.5 hours

DIFFICULTY Challenging—exposed edges and varying terrain; watch littles

SEASON Year-round. Fall has great foliage.

GET THERE From Thomaston, take Highway 6 south 1 mile to the Black Rock State Park turnoff—pass the turnoff, and in just 200 feet, you'll see a small pullout on the west side of the highway with a blue Mattatuck Trail sign; the unmarked trailhead is across the street.

Google Maps: bit.ly/timberleatherman

RESTROOMS Down the road at Black Rock State Park (none at trailhead)

FEE None

TREAT YOURSELF Try a famous mini strawberry Boston cream pie, donut, or bagel breakfast sandwich at Tony's Coffee Express a few minutes north.

Mattatuck State Forest, Connecticut Department of Energy and Environmental Protection | (860) 567-5694
Instagram @CT.Deep | Facebook @CTDeep

famous blue blazes of the Connecticut Forest and Park Association (CFPA) up the hillside, sometimes heading up steep inclines—take your time and keep an eye out for a blaze every 50 feet or so. You'll cross several ledges good for power-ups, including Crane's Lookout just under a mile from the road, and take in the view of the surrounding Mattatuck State Forest on the historic homeland of the Mohican. At a junction with the Jericho Trail, turn left and find the cave. Follow the blue blazes on the rock to explore where the Leatherman camped years ago. *Mattatuck* is derived from the Algonquin name, Matetacoke, which means, "a place without trees." Early colonial towns and industry needed fuel, so the trees around here were all cut down. Luckily, in the 1930s, the Civilian Conservation Corps reforested the area. You'll pass through their new-growth trees as you make your way back to your car. Consider staying the night and camping at Black Rock State Park.

SCAVENGER HUNT

Legend of the Leatherman

For nearly thirty years, until his death in 1889, the Leatherman would complete a 360-mile circuit every 34 days—walking roughly 10 miles a day. Along the way, he tended gardens and stored food in caves like this one. He didn't speak English and not much of his background is known, but towns-people would await his punctual arrival every month. How many days in a row could you hike for?

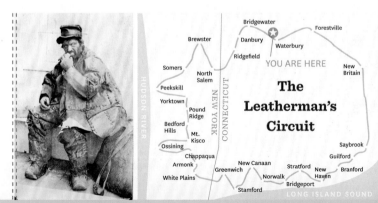

Portrait of the vagabond hiker; how long would it take you to hike the Leatherman's route? >

The Leatherman's Circuit

YOU ARE HERE

Bridgewater · Forestville · Brewster · Danbury · Waterbury · Ridgefield · New Britain · Somers · North Salem · Peekskill · Yorktown · Pound Ridge · Bedford Hills · Mt. Kisco · Ossining · Chappaqua · Armonk · Greenwich · New Canaan · Stratford · New Haven · Branford · Guilford · Saybrook · Norwalk · Bridgeport · White Plains · Stamford

HUDSON RIVER · NEW YORK · CONNECTICUT · LONG ISLAND SOUND

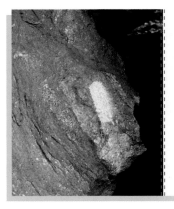

Blue blaze

Since 1929, the Connecticut Forest and Park Association has created and maintained a network of trails marked with sky blue paint. See if you can recognize the different patterns for turning left or right and the end of the trail. How many steps do you count between each blaze?

< Follow the blazes

Northern red oak

See if you can spot these pointy leaves on your hike. The deciduous red oak drops its leaves every fall—trace one in your nature journal. Are you here in springtime? These are monoecious trees, meaning the male and female flowers are on the same branch. The catkins, those stringy hanging flowers, are male. Can you spot the red female flowers that create acorns in fall?

Quercus rubra leaves and catkin >

Sassafras

It's hard not to smile at these leaves, which can be shaped like mittens or have three-lobed "fingers." Use a leaf from the ground to high-five a buddy, then smell your hand. Sassafras can be an ingredient in root beer (the raw plant is poisonous to eat though). When the leaves change color in fall, count how many shades of yellow, orange, and red you find.

< Three-lobed *Sassafras albidum* leaves

3

BOULDER AROUND BURR POND

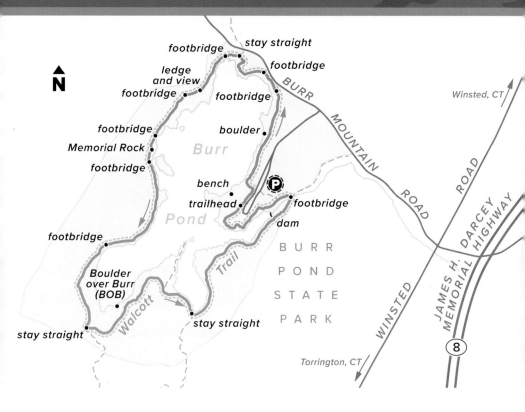

footbridge
stay straight
ledge and view
footbridge
footbridge
footbridge
BURR
Winsted, CT
MOUNTAIN ROAD
footbridge
boulder
Memorial Rock
Burr
footbridge
bench
trailhead
footbridge
Pond
dam
footbridge
BURR POND STATE PARK
Trail
Boulder over Burr (BOB)
Walcott
stay straight
stay straight
WINSTED
JAMES H. MEMORIAL
DARCEY HIGHWAY
ROAD
8
Torrington, CT
N

YOUR ADVENTURE

Adventurers, you're on the historic homeland of the Mohican. In 1857, Burr Pond was the site of the world's first condensed milk factory, which helped feed the Union Army during the Civil War. From the beach near the parking area, you'll walk counterclockwise on plank walkways through wetlands and a former beaver dam. You'll come upon a large boulder with

LENGTH

2.6-mile

loop

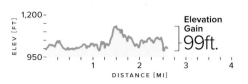

1,200-

ELEV [FT]

950-

Elevation Gain 99ft.

DISTANCE [MI]

1   2   3   4

HIKE + EXPLORE 2 hours

DIFFICULTY Moderate—rooty, but mostly flat with no exposed ledges

SEASON Year-round. Great for snowshoes or skis in winter; January brings No Child Left Inside's annual winter festival; great for a swim in summer.

GET THERE From CT-8, take exit 46 to Burrville and turn left on Burr Mountain Road after half a mile. After 1 mile, turn left on Pond Road to enter the park.

Google Maps: bit.ly/timberburr

RESTROOMS At parking lot

FEE Free for CT residents; nonresidents free on weekdays, $15 on weekends

TREAT YOURSELF Peaches 'N Cream, just 15 minutes south on CT-8, has seasonal scoops like blueberry and pumpkin.

Burr Pond State Park,
Connecticut Department of Energy
and Environmental Protection
(860) 482-1817
Instagram @CT.Deep
Facebook @CTDeep

How many different trees can you see at the water's edge?

a plaque honoring a former trail builder and cross a few more footbridges before coming upon the BOB (Boulder over Burr)—a great power-up stop. When you start up again you'll pass the John Muir Trail on the right—keep going straight. You'll also pass a blue- and yellow-blazed trail to your left that goes to a lake viewpoint, which is a fun bonus if you have the energy. Keep going and you'll pass the other end of the John Muir Trail on the right. You'll know you're near the end of the loop when you happen upon the dam—farmer Milo Burr dammed the streams here in 1851 to power mills in Torrington. Walk around the dam until you're back to the beach.

SCAVENGER HUNT

BOB (Boulder over Burr)

Peer up at this 15-foot-tall glacial erratic boulder (from the Latin *errare*, which means "to wander") made of granitic gneiss. As a glacier moves, it can break off pieces of bedrock and transport them great distances in a process called plucking.

Can you find BOB's "face"? There are nearly forty glacial erratics along this trail—how many can you count?

Take a break under the overhang of this special boulder >

Seasonal special: serviceberry

This plant's white flowers are some of the first to bloom in spring. Early colonists would wait for the flowers to appear before holding funeral services for loved ones who had died during the cold winter—their arrival meant the ground had thawed enough to dig a burial hole. The flowers turn into purple berries around June.

< *Amelanchier*

Phil Buttrick Memorial Rock

Phil was a Civilian Conservation Corps forester who camped with a team right in this spot in the 1930s. Find the memorial plaque on the side of the rock and think about when Phil led the team to build this very trail. What steps do you think it takes to build a trail?

< Can you find the plaque on the huge boulder?

Dam

Burr Pond is man-made. Milo Burr dammed several creeks with this structure in 1851 to generate power for a tannery (which makes leather) and sawmills. Those buildings are gone, but the dam remains. Construct your own dam near the water's edge and test its strength with a scoop from the lake.

Watch the water fall into the pond ↗

Seasonal special: mountain laurel

Though you can spot its leathery evergreen leaves any time of year, from May to June you'll find Connecticut's state flower blooming all along this trail. Look closely at its clusters of white-and-pink flowers. Tear a small piece of paper from your nature journal—can you fold it to look like the closed buds?

< *Kalmia latifolia* (in Latin, *latifolia* means "broad-leaved")

4

DO SOME RECON ON MOUNT TOM TOWER

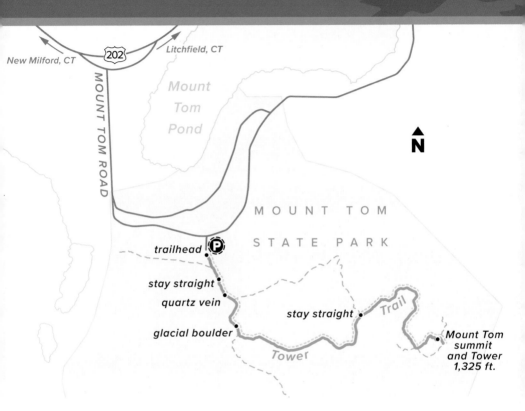

YOUR ADVENTURE

Adventurers, today you can imagine you're the king or queen of your own tower overlooking the historic homelands of the Mohican and Paugussett. This is one of Connecticut's first state parks, created when philanthropist Charles H. Senff donated the land in 1911. From the parking area, pass the Tower Trail sign at the flat start and follow the yellow blazes to where the

ELEV (FT)

1,400–

900–

Elevation
Gain
336ft.

DISTANCE (MI)

1   2   3   4

LENGTH **1.3 miles** out and back

HIKE + EXPLORE 1.5 hours

DIFFICULTY Moderate—rocky, rooty, and
uphill, but it's short and doable

SEASON Year-round. Weekends get busy;
consider arriving early.

GET THERE From Highway 202 east of
Litchfield, turn south on Old CT-25, then take
an immediate left on Mount Tom Road for
0.3 miles to the yellow gate and Tower sign.

Google Maps: bit.ly/timbermttom

RESTROOMS At main parking lot by the pond

FEE Free for CT residents all days, $15 weekend
and holiday charge for nonresidents

TREAT YOURSELF Seasonal ice cream at
Arethusa Farm Dairy, just off 202 near Litchfield.

Mount Tom State Park,
Connecticut Department of Energy
and Environmental Protection
(860) 567-8870 Memorial Day to Labor Day
weekends, (860) 567-2592 weekdays, and
(860) 868-2592 September to May
Instagram @CT.Deep | Facebook @CTDeep

∧ Ready to climb?

trail gets rocky. You'll pass two smaller spur trails and a huge boulder before the climbing begins—pass all the side trails and stay straight to reach the former fire lookout tower. Climb the stairs, power up or stop for lunch, and make your way back down the way you came.

SCAVENGER HUNT

Climb the tower

This 34-foot-high observation tower was built in 1921 out of black metamorphic (changed with heat and pressure over time) gneiss to replace a wooden tower built in 1888 on the same spot. It's one of Connecticut's over forty original lookout towers. Maybe one day you'll climb a few of the others! Make up a story to tell your hiking buddy about someone who uses this tower. Who are they and what do they do here?

Count the 45 steps to the top >

∧ A clear day reveals several summits in the distance

Tower view

Do a 360 on top of the tower—can you spot Bear Mountain to the north? It's on the border with Massachusetts. Look east for Bantam Lake, west for New York's Catskill Mountains, and south for Long Island Sound. Take out your nature journal to sketch what you see. Use a compass (like the one on your phone) and be sure to mark north, east, south, and west.

Sensitive fern

This fern is sensitive—it withers in the cold or when it doesn't get enough water. What are you sensitive to? Look among the green fronds to find its smaller fertile fronds covered with brown beads—these release spores that help the fern reproduce.

< Onoclea sensibilis

Quartz vein in gneiss

Look at the map of the glacier's retreat. Can you tell how long ago the ice left this area? Try to imagine a sheet of ice taller than a skyscraper, covering everything you see. How do you think the land looked different after it melted? Kneel down to trace the white quartz veins through the gneiss (named for an old German word meaning "sparkling"). As the glacier moved over Connecticut, fine-grained sand and pebbles frozen to its bottom scraped and polished these rocks like a giant piece of sandpaper. Have you ever polished something smooth like this? Maybe a piece of wood or your fingernails?

These smooth rocks were polished by a glacier >

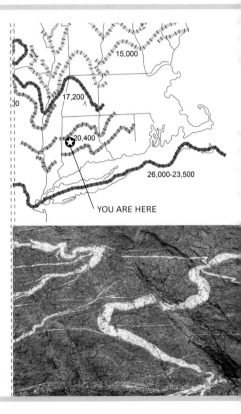

15,000

17,200

20,400

26,000-23,500

YOU ARE HERE

5

CLIMB DOWN TO CAMPBELL FALLS

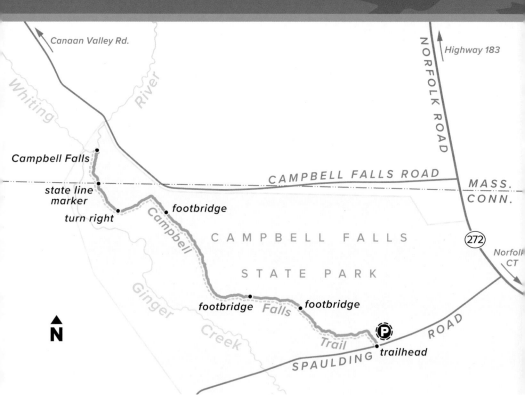

YOUR ADVENTURE

Adventurers, today you get to explore the northernmost hike in Connecticut and—bonus!—hike in two different states. You'll start off in Connecticut on the historic homeland of the Mohican. After crossing a few small footbridges, you'll reach a concrete state line marker where you can jump back and forth between Massachusetts and Connecticut. How many times can

ELEV [FT]

1,200–

950–

Elevation Gain
169ft.

DISTANCE [MI]

1   2   3

∧ **Power up at each bridge and look carefully for something cool underneath**

LENGTH

1 mile out and back

HIKE + EXPLORE 1 hour

DIFFICULTY Moderate—rooty, but mostly flat until final descent; short

SEASON Year-round. Spring has great waterfall flows.

GET THERE From Norfolk, head north on CT-272 for 4 miles and turn left on Spaulding Road. The small parking lot will be on your right after a quarter mile.

Google Maps: bit.ly/timbercampbellfalls

RESTROOMS None

FEE None

TREAT YOURSELF Just 10 minutes south is the Berkshire Country Store, where you can grab yummy to-go deli and breakfast sandwiches for your power-ups.

Campbell Falls State Park Reserve, Connecticut Department of Energy and Environmental Protection
(860) 482-1817
Instagram @CT.Deep | Facebook @CTDeep

you jump before getting tired? Keep going on the trail, and it will start to descend. Stay to the right, and you'll shortly find yourself at the 50-mile-long Whiting River where a 60-foot two-tiered waterfall awaits. Take time to play on the rocks, power up, and think about why entrepreneur John Campbell might have wanted to operate a mill here before the Revolutionary War. Head back the way you came.

SCAVENGER HUNT

Campbell Falls

Zig and zag—check out the Whiting River as it makes its way through the granitic gneiss (granite changed by heat and pressure). It is still eroding the rocks in its path today. How many different colors of rock can you find at the base of the falls?

< The river carved out this gorge to form a two-tiered waterfall

Rock polypody

Once you arrive at the falls, look between rocks for this fern. Its leaves are pinnate, which means divided along a common line like a feather (*pinnate* comes from the Latin word for feather). This fern's leaves only divide once, so they look like little fingers. Are they bigger or smaller than your little fingers?

Polypodium virginianum >

Orange mycena

These small, wispy, gilled mushrooms like to hang out in clusters on logs. Take a moment to search for some. Make like a mycologist— someone who studies mushrooms—and sketch one in your nature journal.

< Summer through fall, you might spy *Mycena leaiana* after a rain

Evergreen wood fern

These common ferns look lacy because their fronds divide three different times. First there's the main blade with two leaflets that split off that, then each leaflet splits off that, and—look close—one more tiny split. Count how many leaflets are on one frond and compare numbers with a hiking buddy.

Dryopteris intermedia >

Rippled rock

Imagine these rocks once buried way below the Earth's surface, where pressure (from miles of rock above) and heat cooked and transformed them over millions of years to create granitic gneiss. Check out the ripples— soft minerals within the rock have been slowly weathered out to make this pattern.

< Look for pieces of ripply granitic gneiss below the falls

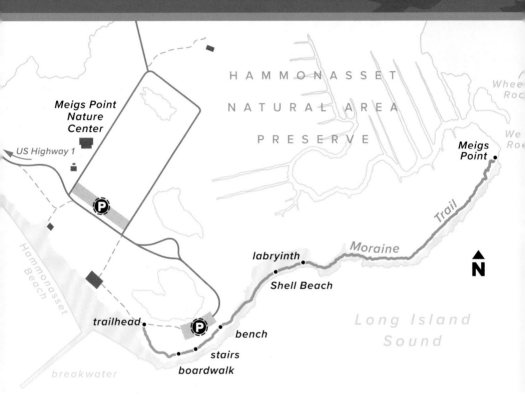

HAMMONASSET NATURAL AREA PRESERVE

Meigs Point Nature Center

US Highway 1

Meigs Point

labryinth

Moraine

Trail

Shell Beach

Long Island Sound

trailhead

bench

stairs

boardwalk

breakwater

Hammonasset Beach

N

Whee Roc

We Ro

YOUR ADVENTURE

Adventurers, welcome to the historic homelands of the Hammonasset, Quinnipiac, and Wappinger. This area was once used for farming—the name Hammonasset means "where we dig holes in the ground." Today, you'll travel along a recessional moraine, a pile of rocks and sediment left behind by a melting glacier. You might want to bring some binoculars— over 300 bird species pass through here throughout the year. See how many

LENGTH

1.1 miles

out and back

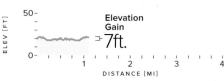

50-

ELEV [FT]

Elevation
Gain

⇨ 7ft.

0-

1   2   3   4

DISTANCE [MI]

HIKE + EXPLORE 1 hour

DIFFICULTY Easy—flat and short; plenty to see and places to stop and play

SEASON Year-round.

GET THERE Take Highway 450 south through Madison for 2 miles. Merge onto Hammonasset Con, take the third exit at the traffic circle, and turn left into the Nature Center parking lot.

Google Maps: bit.ly/timbermeigs

RESTROOMS At parking lot

FEE Free for CT residents; $22 weekends, $14 weekdays, $7 after 4 p.m. for nonresidents

TREAT YOURSELF Try New Haven–style pizza at Grand Apizza, just 4 miles west— open since 1955!

Hammonasset Beach State Park, Connecticut Department of Energy and Environmental Protection
(203) 245-2785
Instagram @CT.Deep
Facebook @CTDeep

Ready to explore the longest beach in Connecticut?

different species you can spot. After walking to the beach from the Nature Center, pick up the trail and cross a boardwalk—take in the view of Long Island Sound and power up. You'll head down the stairs and pass a bench before landing on Shell Beach. Here empty mollusk shells tink against each other as the tide goes in and out, creating a "singing" beach. Farther along, you'll find a labyrinth—a spiral of shells and rocks leading toward a peaceful center. Walk through it and think of something positive. Finally, end at Meigs Point, where you can bird-watch and look for West Rock and Wheeler Rock. Head back the way you came and consider camping at the park's 500-spot campground.

SCAVENGER HUNT

Seasonal special: harbor seals

These mammals migrate through here mid-November to December, and you can see them hauling out on the sand or West Rock for a rest— be sure to give them space. Watch them go underwater—they can stay under for forty minutes and dive up  to 1500 feet looking for fish to snack on. How deep can you dive?

Phoca vitulina ⌐

Slipper shells

Look closely at the musical shells on Shell Beach—they look like little slippers. Put them on your fingers and take them for a walk. Imagine living in a colony made up of snails in shells like these packed close together on the rocks. What do you think life would be like?

< *Crepidula fornicata*

Common sanddragon

Look for this water-loving dragonfly hovering like a helicopter with its four long wings and yellow and black markings. It can fly up to 30 miles per hour and see in all directions at once with its huge, domelike eyes. How many directions can your eyes see if you don't move your head?

Progomphus obscurus >

Seasonal special: bull thistle

From June to September, look for this pink flower on top of a spiky green ball (the ball is the thistle's fruit). If pollinated, the flower will turn into thistledown, seeds with fluffy fibers that help them float on the wind. If you find thistledown, give it a blow (be careful of the spikes) and make a wish.

Cirsium vulgare >

Herring gull

Juvenile (young) birds are brown, but after four years, they get a bright white chest and head and gray wings. Sit and watch their behavior for a few minutes, writing anything you notice in your nature journal. If you catch them dropping something from high in the sky, it's probably a shellfish they're trying to break open so they can eat what's inside. Smart!

Larus argentatus (in Latin, *argentatus* means "decorated with silver") >

7

SEE WHAT'S COOKIN' AT THE DEVIL'S HOPYARD

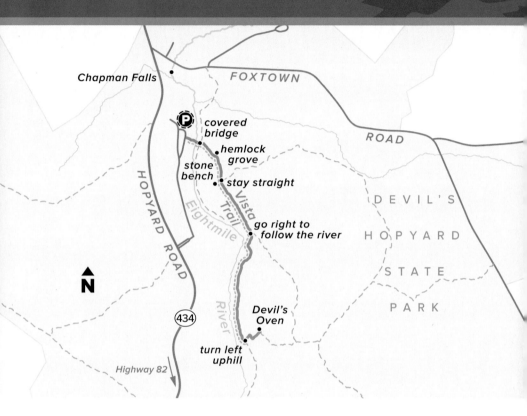

YOUR ADVENTURE

Adventurers, you'll kick off this adventure on the historic homeland of the Mohegan by crossing the Eightmile River. Though actually 14 miles long, the Eightmile gets its name because it meets the Connecticut River 8 miles upstream from the Long Island Sound. Imagine lumber being shipped down this river to sawmills in the 1800s. Start your hike on the orange-blazed

LENGTH

1 mile

out and back

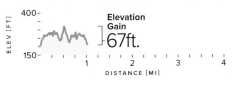

Elevation Gain

67ft.

HIKE + EXPLORE 1 hour

DIFFICULTY Moderate—mainly flat, lots of roots, and a scramble up to the Oven

SEASON Year-round. Be careful on icy or snowy winter days.

GET THERE From Highway 85 south of Salem, turn west on Highway 82 for 5 miles and north on Highway 434 for 2 miles until you see the park entrance on the right.

Google Maps: bit.ly/timberdevilsoven

RESTROOMS At parking lot

FEE None

TREAT YOURSELF In spring and summer, try the Muddy Hooves cone at Salem Valley Farms, just a few miles to the east.

Devil's Hopyard State Park,
Connecticut Department of Energy
and Environmental Protection
(860) 424-3200
Instagram @CT.Deep
Facebook @CTDeep

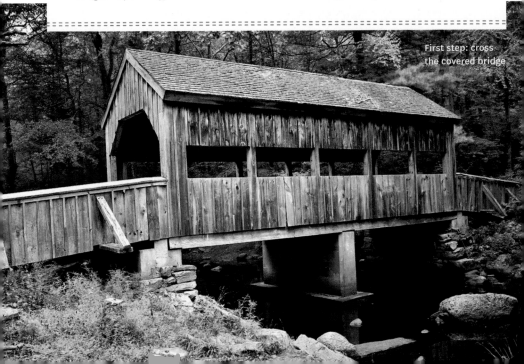

First step: cross the covered bridge

Vista Trail, and take a quick power up at the stone bench. Stay right at the trail junction, and then right at the next one, too, staying close to the river the whole time. Finally, come upon a sign for Devil's Oven; take some deep breaths and carefully make the short scramble up to this cave. Power up with some lunch and invent your own legend for the park. Why do you think it's called Devil's Hopyard? Farmers used to grow hops for beer here, and legend has it that a devil created some of the geological shapes and waterfalls by stomping around. Head back the way you came to check out Chapman Falls and consider relaxing for the night at the campground.

SCAVENGER HUNT

Eastern hemlock

You can often tell a hemlock from its tiny little cones, one of the smallest in the conifer (cone-producing) world. They hang off the ends of branches like little ornaments. If you find one on the ground, break its scales open. Sometimes they are closed to keep the seeds safe, and sometimes they're open to let them go.

< *Tsuga canadensis*

Fly agaric mushroom

These speckled toadstools look like they came straight from a fairytale. Find them under trees after a summer or fall rain. Look at the warts along its cap and peek underneath at its gills. Try not to touch it—it's poisonous!

Amanita muscaria can be brown
(like this one) or bright red >

Devil's Oven

Devil's Oven is a small schist and gneiss cave that is over 400 million years old. Be careful as you climb up to approach it—instead of going inside, make yourself a hemlock cone "pizza" and cook it in the Oven. Caves like this are created when some parts of a rock erode before others—it's called differential weathering. Look up and around for other evidence of weathering.

This cave is 3 feet wide and goes 15 feet back >

Covered bridge

Covered bridges aren't just cool, they're also smart—wooden bridges that are covered last longer because the important supports are protected from

rain and snow. This covered bridge was first built in 1937 and lasted until a flood in 1982 destroyed it. It was rebuilt in 1986—how long do you think it will last this time? Maybe you can come back every year to check on it.

< The view from inside

Eightmile River

This part of the river empties into the lower Connecticut River at Hamburg Cove. This is a special place—New England has 65,000 miles of river, but less than one percent are included in the US Fish and Wildlife Service's Wild and Scenic Rivers Program.

What do you think this special classification might mean?

Listen to the babbling of the Eightmile along your hike ⌐

8

RELAX ON INDIAN CHAIR AT MASHAMOQUET BROOK

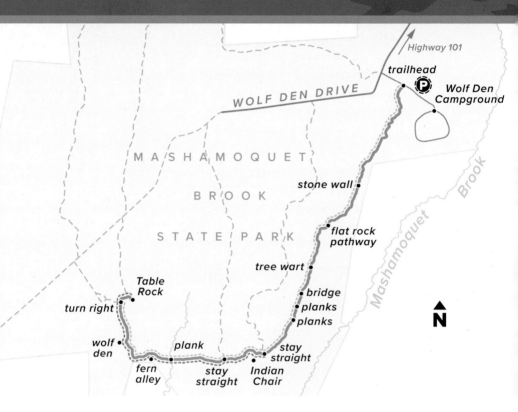

YOUR ADVENTURE

Adventurers, today you'll explore the historic homeland of the Nipmuc in search of three rock structures within Mashamoquet ("stream of good fishing") Brook State Park. From the parking lot, follow the blue blazes on a trail that starts flat. Be sure to power up at the old 3-foot-tall agricultural stone wall; soon after, the trail begins to roll up and down with lots of roots

LENGTH

2.8 miles

out and back

Elevation Gain
315ft.

ELEV [FT] · 700 · 200

DISTANCE [MI]

HIKE + EXPLORE 2 hours

DIFFICULTY Challenging—rocky, rooty, and lots of uphill, but worth it for three awesome features

SEASON Year-round. Great fall colors.

GET THERE Take Highway 44 south from Pomfret, then turn left onto Highway 101 and make a quick right onto Wolf Den Drive. The visitor center and parking lot will be on your left after 0.8 miles.

Google Maps bit.ly/timberwolfsden

RESTROOMS At parking lot

FEE None

TREAT YOURSELF Just a few miles west on Highway 97, We-Li-Kit Farm has fresh maple syrup and homemade ice cream.

Mashamoquet Brook State Park,
Connecticut Department of Energy
and Environmental Protection
(860) 928-6121
Instagram @CT.Deep
Facebook @CTDeep

A great power-up stop halfway along the trail

and rocks. After a bridge and a plank walk, you'll push up the hillside and find the Indian Chair (pay careful attention to the blazes, it's just a teensy bit off the trail to your left). Power up and take in the view from the stone sofa. Continue your uphill push on the red-and-blue trail—hike past two junctions, passing red trails going to the right as you stay straight on blue until you reach the marked wolf den on the left. Just a little farther on, you'll find a small, signed red side trail heading right down to the very flat Table Rock, which just begs you to have lunch on it. Turn back the way you came and consider camping at Wolf Den Campground when you're done.

SCAVENGER HUNT

Pignut hickory

Look up at this deciduous (leaf-dropping) tree to see its beautiful five-pointed clusters of leaves with serrated (jagged) edges. In late summer and fall, you can find its fruit—a green husk with ridges like a pumpkin, which breaks open to reveal a brown nut with a "nose" like a pig.

< *Carya glabra* (in Latin, "nut-bearing" and "smooth")

Millipede

Have a look on the ground for this slow-moving invertebrate (an animal with no backbone). Try to count its legs—but don't touch! If picked up or threatened, it emits a stinky liquid. Millipedes are part of a class called Diplopoda (*diplo* means "double" and *poda* is another word for "feet") and have two pairs of legs for each body segment—

centipedes, their distant cousins, have only one pair per body segment.

Even though *milli* means "thousand" and *pede* means "feet," most millipedes only have a couple hundred feet ⌐

The wolf den

Imagine it's 1742, there's one wolf left in the whole state, and it keeps eating your sheep. Israel Putnam and his neighbors wanted to protect their flocks, so one night they followed the wolf to this very den. Putnam tied a rope around his ankle and had his neighbors hold the end while he went inside. He crawled over 40 feet in before he found the wolf and shot it. His neighbors then dragged them both out with the rope. Old Put later became a famous general in the Continental Army during the Revolutionary War, and the story of how he killed the last wolf in Connecticut was told many times.

ʌ Peer carefully into the den; Israel Putnam, or "Old Put"

Table Rock

Feel the smoothness of this 400-million-year-old slab made from metamorphic Canterbury gneiss. Count its whitish lichen patches. Lichens are made of algae and fungi working together in a symbiotic (helpful to both) relationship. Draw the rock and its lichen patches in your nature journal.

< Long, flat, and smooth—perfect for a power-up

Indian Chair

Try to get your whole family on this rocky chair. It's made of Canterbury gneiss, a metamorphic rock (changed by intense heat and pressure). Look at the seat's straight surfaces and imagine ice freezing and thawing, over and over, until it cut this shape.

< Take a seat

ADVENTURES IN
RHODE ISLAND

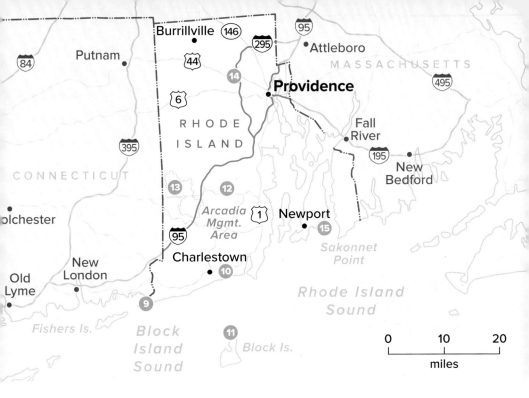

Adventurers, we're heading east from Connecticut to enter the Ocean State, the smallest state in our country. Rhode Island was named by Dutch explorer Adriaen Block, who described it as Roodt Eylandt ("red island" in Dutch) because of its red clay. What name would you give this area? From the coastal lowlands and major islands offshore to the eastern uplands with their (slightly) higher elevation—the highest point in the state is Jerimoth Hill at 812 feet— you'll see evidence of the same glacier that covered Connecticut. Look for stone walls, old mill dams, towpaths, and river canals from the Industrial Revolution as you explore gorgeous beaches, historical forts, rockeries, waterfalls, ponds, and too many footbridges to count. You'll encounter lands managed by wildlife refuges and conservancies, the Audubon Society, and Rhode Island State Parks, and have the opportunity to become a master bird-watcher. As you drive or take a ferry to your next hike, reflect on the state motto: "hope." What is something you are hopeful for on your next adventure?

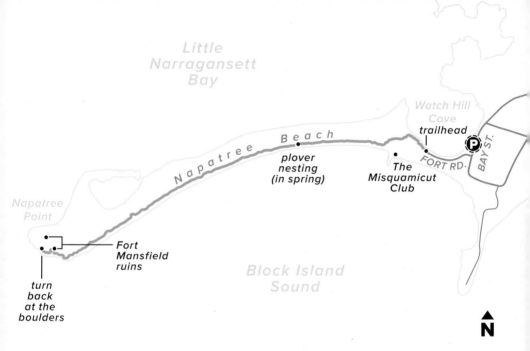

Little Narragansett Bay

Watch Hill Cove

trailhead

Napatree Beach

plover nesting (in spring)

The Misquamicut Club

FORT RD.

BAY ST.

Napatree Point

Fort Mansfield ruins

Block Island Sound

turn back at the boulders

N

YOUR ADVENTURE

Adventurers, you're about to travel along a strip of sand on the historic homelands of the Niantic and Pequot. Dutch explorer Adriaen Block named this southwesternmost point of Rhode Island "Nap of Trees" because it used to be covered in thick forest. Make your way along the beach, looking for treasures left behind by the tide and watching for interesting birds—this

LENGTH

3 miles

out and back

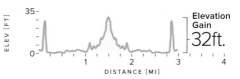

ELEV [FT]

35–

0–

Elevation Gain

32ft.

DISTANCE [MI]

1   2   3   4

HIKE + EXPLORE 1.5 hours

DIFFICULTY Moderate—flat along the beach, but 3 miles in sand can feel long for short legs

SEASON Year-round. Great in summer and fall for smaller crowds as the shore-birds and raptors stage for migration.

GET THERE From Westerly, take Route 1A/ Watch Hill Road and follow it as it turns into Wauwinnet Avenue and Bay Street. Turn right into Larkin Square and park outside the yacht club. Walk through the parking lot and north onto the beach.

Google Maps: bit.ly/timbernapatree

RESTROOMS None

FEE 2 hours of free parking in Watch Hill; paid parking is also available

TREAT YOURSELF Pompelmo Gelateria has yummy, seasonal gelato cones. Bonus: it's right next to the parking lot.

Napatree Point Conservation Area,
The Watch Hill Conservancy
(401) 315-5399
Instagram @TheWatchHillConservancy
Facebook @NapatreePoint

The spit is a perfect spot to watch the birds and the sunset is considered a globally Important Bird Area (IBA). When you reach the end of the spit (an extended finger of sandy coast formed by wind), look up on the hill for a small trail. Carefully scramble up to find Fort Mansfield. Enjoy the view of the old foundation from afar and try to think why the military abandoned it. Take in the view, head back down, and power up at the boulders that mark the end of this hike. Be sure to check yourselves for ticks. Imagine a hurricane blowing through here in 1938 and completely reshaping the coast, creating Sandy Point Island and wiping away over forty buildings. Go back the way you came and consider staying for a beautiful sunset.

SCAVENGER HUNT

Fort Mansfield

In 1898, the Army and Navy worked together to build a series of defensive forts all along the East Coast. Fort Mansfield, named after the Civil War major general Joseph Mansfield, opened in 1901. During a mock battle in 1907, it became clear the fort was open to attack, so the government eventually sold it to a summer resort.

< The foundation of Fort Mansfield is all that's left

Beach rose

Look for this short shrub with toothy, egg-shaped leaves growing above the sandy shoreline. Its pink, spring-blooming flowers are beautiful, but it can be invasive. Look at how much shoreline it covers!

Rosa rugosa >

Seasonal special: American oystercatcher

Look for this black-and-white shorebird in springtime—you can't miss its long, bright orange, chopstick-like beak. Why do you think their beaks are shaped this way? If you spot one breaking into shells on the beach, the answer should become clear.

Haematopus palliatus >

Osprey platforms

Starting in spring, you might find these raptors using the man-made nesting platforms in the dune grass to lay their eggs and take care of fledglings. Recognize them by their white heads with a brown stripe through the eye, or, when flying overhead, their brown-and-white-striped wings with spread-out "fingertip" feathers.

∧ *Pandion haliaetus* (Pandion was a mythical Greek king and *haliaetus* means "fishing eagle")

Endangered piping plover

Spring through midsummer is nesting season, so some areas might be fenced off to protect these endangered shorebirds. Their feathers were once harvested for fancy hats, which reduced their population. Even though they aren't hunted anymore, the plovers are still protected because they need to lay their eggs in the open sand, where they're in danger from hikers, dogs, and other predators. The Watch Hill Conservancy helps protect and count plover fledglings each year.

∧ *Charadrius melodus*

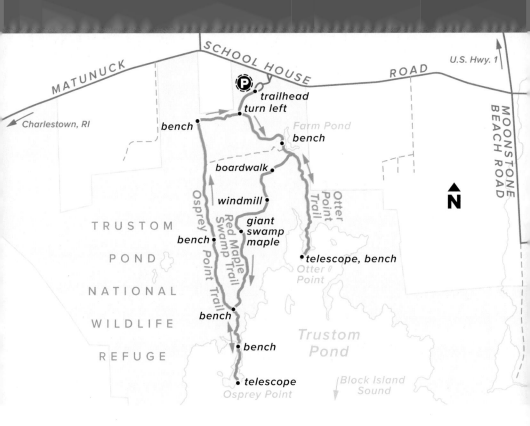

YOUR ADVENTURE

Adventurers, you're heading to the historic homeland of the Narragansett and the only undeveloped coastal salt pond in Rhode Island today. Check out the wildlife siting board for species you might see and head out on the wide gravel path. Take your first left onto the Otter Point Trail and stop at the two observation platforms at Farm Pond to look for any wildlife and try

LENGTH

2.5-mile

loop

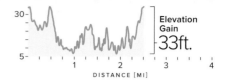

HIKE + EXPLORE 1.5 hours

DIFFICULTY Easy—little elevation gain and a fairly level trail

SEASON Year-round. Spring and fall are great for catching migrating birds; pond freezes over in winter. Can be buggy, so consider bug repellent; beware of ticks.

GET THERE Take Matunuck School House Road 3 miles east of Charlestown. The parking lot is on the south side of the road.

Google Maps: bit.ly/timbertrustom

RESTROOMS At parking lot

FEE None

TREAT YOURSELF Don't miss Daddy's Bread, just a minute east on Matunuck School House Road, for a blueberry muffin or apple cinnamon bread—it's an honor system, so grab your treats, pay with cash or online payment, and leave happy.

Trustom Pond National Wildlife Refuge
(401) 364-9124
Facebook @RInwrc

A bench overlooking the pond makes a great power-up spot

to count the lily pads. Keep going until you reach Otter Point, where you can power up on the bench and use the telescope to spot some of the many birds migrating through during spring and fall. Head back the way you came and turn left onto Red Maple Swamp Trail, crossing a boardwalk, passing an old windmill, and eventually turning left to reach beautiful Osprey Point—can you see Block Island Sound beyond the pond? On the way back, stay straight onto Osprey Point Trail then return on the grassy Farm Field Loop Trail—how many different kinds of grasses do you see? Take a final left, stop at a couple benches, and return to the trailhead.

SCAVENGER HUNT

White-tailed deer

Go into "quiet mode" for three minutes or more as you walk, listening for the footsteps of the only deer native to Rhode Island. Look for its tracks with two heart-shaped cloves (toes).

< Odocoileus virginianus

Double-crested cormorant

Watch for this dark black bird near the water. It is a diving bird, but its feathers aren't waterproof, so you'll often spot it standing with its wings spread out to dry after fishing. Draw its shape in your nature journal and use your brightest orange for the bare skin on its face.

Phalacrocorax auritus >

Mute swan

These swans were introduced to New England from Europe because people thought they were pretty. They aren't actually completely silent, but they are quieter than our native swans. The park has struggled with keeping a balance between this species and other birds that live here. Watch its behavior for at least five minutes—what do you notice? Compare your observations with a hiking buddy.

Cygnus olor ⌐

Snapping turtle

At the pond, keep an eye out for this mud-loving reptile. Check out its powerful, beak-like jaws and imagine them snapping shut on dinner. Show your hiking partner your best snapper impression.

< *Chelydra serpentina* (how do you think it got the name *serpentina*?)

Seasonal special: skunk cabbage

Most of the year, you might not notice this plant, but it will get your attention in springtime. Does the unusual look of its purple flowers (with a hood called a spathe covering a spike called a spadix) make up for the way they smell like rotten meat? What kind of pollinators do you think this attracts? Make a poem about how the flowers smell to you.

Symplocarpus foetidus >

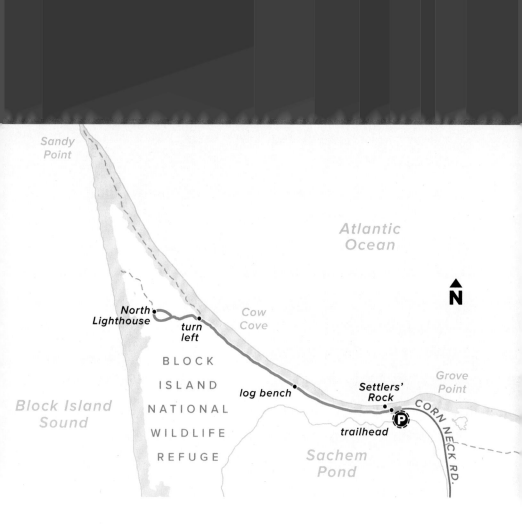

YOUR ADVENTURE

Adventurers, today you're adventuring on Block Island, historic homeland of the Manissean. The Narragansett Indians who lived on the mainland named the island Manisses, which translates to "Island of the Little God," but Dutch explorer Adriaen Block later named it for himself. You'll start at Settlers' Rock and walk along the beach. Be sure to keep your eyes peeled

LENGTH

1.2 miles

out and back

Elevation Gain
32ft.

ELEV [FT] 35– 0–

DISTANCE [MI] 1 2 3 4

HIKE + EXPLORE 1 hour

DIFFICULTY Easy—flat and level, though sand can get tiring for little legs

SEASON Year-round. Spring and fall are great for spotting migrating birds.

GET THERE This super-adventure requires a ferry ride, but it's so worth it! From Point Judith, a traditional 55-minute ferry runs year-round several times a day and is the only ferry that carries vehicles.

Express ferries (no vehicles) depart from Point Judith, Newport, and Fall River, MA, during spring and summer. If you want to bring your car, it's essential to book a reservation early at blockislandferry.com— they open reservations every January. If you prefer to just take yourselves on the ferry, you don't need a reservation, and there are taxis and car and bike rentals available on the island. From the ferry dock in New Shoreham, drive/bike/taxi 4 miles north to the end of Corn Neck Road and the parking lot at Settlers' Rock.

Google Maps: bit.ly/timberblock

RESTROOMS None near the hike, so be sure to go at the ferry dock in New Shoreham

FEE None for the trail, but be sure to check ferry and vehicle fees at blockislandferry.com

TREAT YOURSELF Grab a frozen lemonade and a pastry at Aldo's Bakery, just a block from the ferry.

Block Island National Wildlife Refuge
(401) 364-9124 | Facebook @RInwrc

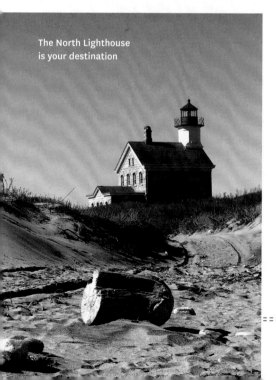

The North Lighthouse is your destination

for one of over seventy species of migratory songbirds that travel here every fall along the Atlantic Flyway in search of warmer waters. You'll soon come upon a small trail heading up the low hill where North Lighthouse sits. Take a moment to make a sand doodle on the high sandbank before reaching the lighthouse, which was built in 1867 and is the fourth lighthouse to stand on this spot. Explore the lighthouse then follow the sand trail down to the beach on Sandy Point. Power up here while you contemplate the three ship-wrecks that happened nearby, then return the way you came.

SCAVENGER HUNT

Beach rose
Look for this shrub with wrinkly green leaves and five-petaled pink flowers that come out in spring. After the flowers fade, they leave behind a bright red "rose hip," a seed pod that looks a bit like a tomato.

< *Rosa rugosa* (in Latin, *rugosa* means "wrinkled")

Beach grass
You'll find this grass in the dunes year-round and its seed heads in summer. If you could look underground, you would see a strong network of connected rhizome roots holding it and other plants together on the coastline, preventing erosion. Blow on the heads to help the seeds spread and continue their good work.

Ammophila breviligulata (in Greek, *ammophila* means "sand friend") >

Settlers' Rock

The first European settlers on Block Island arrived in 1661, bringing with them the island's first cows. Because the cove was too shallow for the settlers' ships to get close to land, they had to push their cows off the ship and make them swim to shore! Sketch in your nature journal the scene of cows swimming ashore.

< Find this memorial at the start of your hike

Blue mussel

Look for these shells along your hike and peek inside. What used to be in here? When mussels are alive, they use tough threads to attach their shells to rocks. It takes a strong predator to pry open a mussel shell to get at the foot, heart, and other organs inside.

< *Mytilus edulis*

North Lighthouse

Imagine you're a lighthouse builder—what important things should you consider before building? The first North Lighthouse was swept out to sea after a couple years, and the second and third versions didn't last long either. This fourth one was built farther from the water and has been here ever since, guiding ships around the dangerous reef that juts out from this point. Can you spot the keeper's quarters?

< Built in 1867, this is Block Island's fourth North Lighthouse

Fisherville Brook

ROAD

Sunderland Rd.

JOSLIN

trailhead

FISHERVILLE

bench

Cedar Swamp Loop Trail

BROOK

bridge

PARDON

bench

WILDLIFE

bridge

bridge

Upper Pond

REFUGE

bench

Split Rock

dam

Split Rock Trail

Widow Sweets Rd., Highway 102

Gardner Cemetery

Pond Trail

bridge

N

YOUR ADVENTURE

Adventurers, today you'll explore the historic homeland of the Narragansett. Start on the blue-blazed Pond Trail, turn right at the yellow blaze to go through the Cedar Swamp Loop, then turn right to get back on the main trail. Cross a bridge over Fisherville Brook and check out Upper Pond,

LENGTH

1.6-mile
loop

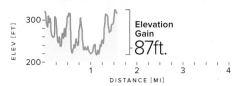

ELEV [FT]

300–

200–

Elevation
Gain
87ft.

DISTANCE [MI]

1   2   3   4

HIKE + EXPLORE 1 hour

DIFFICULTY Easy—flat, gentle terrain

SEASON Year-round. Winter is great for snowshoeing and animal tracks; spring has birds, wildflowers, and frogs; fall has lovely foliage.

GET THERE From Exeter, drive west on Ten Rod Road. Turn north on Widow Sweets Road and right on Pardon Joslin Road. The parking lot will be on the right in just about half a mile.

Google Maps: bit.ly/timberfisherville

RESTROOMS At parking lot

FEE None

TREAT YOURSELF Grab a pizza at Dan's Place, just 6 miles west on Highway 102.

Fisherville Brook Wildlife Refuge,
Audubon Society of Rhode Island
(401) 295-8283
Instagram @RIAudubon
Facebook @AudubonRI

How many frogs can you count on this hike?

making sure to stop and look for frogs. Take the trail to the right to check out the historic cemetery. Head back to the blue blazes and cross another bridge over Fisherville Brook and the dam at the south end of Upper Pond. Keep straight onto orange-blazed Split Rock Trail, counting as many glacial erratic boulders as you can before reaching Split Rock. Power up on any of several benches along the way until you find your way back to the start.

SCAVENGER HUNT

White cedar swamp

Sometimes you can't tell you're in a swamp—it might only be soggy during one season or only soggy under the ground. One way to tell is to look at the plants. Don't you just love bath time? The white cedar does too—it loves growing in swamps. Look for its scaly leaves—how are they different from pine needles? You'll find its light blue berrylike cones in fall. Though small, they can hold up to fifteen seeds each. Count all the cones you see. How many seeds is that?

∧ *Chamaecyparis thyoides*

Gardner Cemetery

This is Rhode Island Historical Cemetery Exeter #93—there are forty burials and twenty-five stones. What is the oldest stone you can find? The most recent? Close your eyes and think a nice thought for these families before you leave.

Pay your respects here >

Upper Pond

L-shaped Upper Pond is the largest pond in the park. It is formed by a dam—when you walk across the bridge you're walking over the dam! On a still day, you can see your reflection in the water like a mirror. In spring and summer, you might even spot a painted turtle sunning on a rock.

< Can you see your reflection in the pond?

Green frog

These diurnal amphibians are active in the daytime, so be sure to look carefully around the bridges by the pond. They've got bright green mouths, like they drank too much lime Kool-Aid, and round tympanums (eardrums) on either side of their heads behind the eyes.

Rana clamitans >

Split Rock

How many glacial erratics can you find on the trail? Many of them came from Canada or New Hampshire or Vermont. The gneiss was formed during a mountain-building event about 450 billion years ago, when the continental plates were shifting and North America got smacked by a piece of land that is now in Africa. Billions of years later, there was a lot of granite and gneiss lying around to be bulldozed or picked up by glaciers and eventually dropped here.

∧ What kind of force split this rock?

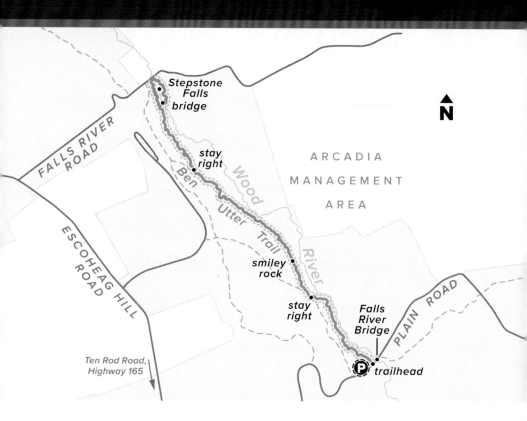

YOUR ADVENTURE

Adventurers, today you're on historic homeland of the Narragansett. You'll
follow the yellow and blue blazes through the lush forest, staying to the
right along the fairly flat Falls River and passing an old gristmill, which
used to grind flour from grain. Keep going, passing a huge smiley boulder—
stop to add your own "eyes" to it and power up for a moment. You'll

LENGTH

3.6 miles
out and back

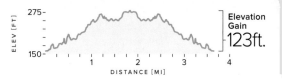

ELEV [FT]

275–

150–

Elevation Gain
123ft.

DISTANCE [MI]

1   2   3   4

HIKE + EXPLORE 2 hours

DIFFICULTY Moderate—on the longer side, with some rocky and rooty terrain

SEASON Year-round. Wildflower blooms and water flow are best in spring; hunting is permitted September through May, so be sure to wear a bright orange hat and top.

GET THERE From Exeter, take Highway 165 west and turn right on Escoheag Hill Road. After a mile, turn right on Plain Road for 1 mile until you see the small pullout and signed gate on the left.

Google Maps: bit.ly/timberstepstone

RESTROOMS None

FEE None

TREAT YOURSELF Just 8 miles south is West's Bakery, famous for their raspberry Bismarks and other pastries.

Arcadia Management Area,
Rhode Island State Parks
(401) 539-2356
Facebook @RIForest

Stepstone Falls drops only 10 feet over its 100-foot length

come upon the blue-and-white trail crossing a bridge to the right, with a blue-blazed road going up—take the blue-and-white trail to the right and cross another small bridge. Keep going until you find the white-blazed River Trail, cross a bridge, and make your final push to the falls over huge boulders. This used to be a rock quarry—look for the chips in the rock. Relax, power up, and turn around to head back the way you came.

SCAVENGER HUNT

Smiley rock

As you add eyes to the giant's smile, check out all the moss and lichen growing on its head. Though they look similar, moss and lichen are from two totally different kingdoms. The dark green moss is a plant—it needs a cool, moist environment to grow. The bright green lichen forms from a partnership between fungi and algae—lichens can grow in much more extreme environments than moss. Examine both closely and draw or write about all the differences you can see.

< Say hello to this friendly giant

Seasonal special: cardinal flower

Look for these showy red flowers in spring-time along the river. Count their five petals and if you find any that have fallen, send a petal boat down the river. These flowers are a favorite of hummingbirds. Sit quietly and watch to see if any fly near.

Lobelia cardinalis >

Seasonal special: yellow marsh marigold

If you visit in April, keep an eye out near bridges for these cheerful yellow blooms. They are one of the first signs of spring and love growing in wet, swampy areas. Members of the buttercup family, they are also known as kingcups. Pretend to be royalty and toast the cups with your water bottle.

< *Caltha palustris*

AMC marker

See if you can find the bridge with this marking from the Appalachian Mountain Club, an organization founded in 1876 that helps protect the land around you. They named this trail after George Benjamin Utter, editor of the local newspaper and developer of the trail network around you. Give the marker a high five to thank the AMC for helping create this trail.

< The Appalachian Mountain Club is the oldest outdoor group in the United States

Seasonal special: black-eyed Susan

In late summer and early fall, you'll find this member of the sunflower family soaking up the sun wherever it can. You can't miss its dark "eyes" against that yellow background. Instead of picking a flower (they have spiky stems!), draw a creature in your nature journal that has black-eyed Susan eyes.

< *Rudbeckia hirta*

PROWL THE POND AT POWDER MILL LEDGES

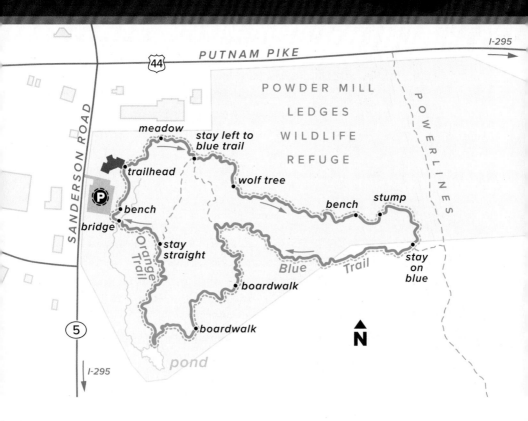

YOUR ADVENTURE

Adventurers, today you're adventuring in a wildlife refuge named for a former gunpowder mill on the historic homelands of the Narragansett and Pauquunaukit. You'll start on the Orange Trail, walking through a large field—keep your eyes open for the bird boxes (and poison ivy). At an orange-and-blue junction, take a left to follow the Blue Trail through the forest. Pass a massive tree and, later on, a bench where you can power up. Come

LENGTH

1.2-mile
loop

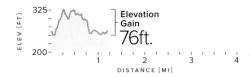

ELEV [FT] 325– 200–

Elevation Gain 76ft.

DISTANCE [MI] 1 2 3 4

HIKE + EXPLORE 1.5 hours

DIFFICULTY Easy—mostly flat

SEASON Year-round. Fall has lovely colors.

GET THERE Turn south from Putnam Pike / Route 44 onto Sanderson Road. The parking lot is the second driveway on your left. Look for the big brown sign.

Google Maps: bit.ly/timberpowdermill

RESTROOMS At visitor center

FEE None

TREAT YOURSELF Scoops, just a mile east on Route 44, serves seasonal ice cream, frozen yogurt, and Allie's famous donuts (cash only).

Powder Mill Ledges Wildlife Refuge, Audubon Society of Rhode Island

(401) 949-5454 | Instagram @RIAudubon

Facebook @AudubonRI

Tons of boardwalks and bridges on this adventure

out of the forest near the power lines and look carefully for the Blue Trail into the forest (not the Yellow Trail to the left that's wide open). Curve back through the forest, passing another small trail on the right, and cross some long boardwalks. Investigate the pond on your left—what plants and animals do you see? Keep going and stay straight, passing the right turn back into the meadow. Cross a bridge, pass another bench, and you'll find yourself back in the meadow where you started. Be sure to hang out for a bit at the Audubon Society National Headquarters before you leave.

SCAVENGER HUNT

Tree swallows

In the first meadow, you can find not just butterflies, beetles, wolf spiders, and dragonflies but also these song-birds, which live here from spring through fall before heading south for winter. They are cavity nesters and love cozy bird boxes. Their song sounds like *chrit, pleet, euree, cheet, chrit, pleet*—sound out the words to sing along with them.

Watch and listen for *Tachycineta bicolor* ↱

Eastern white pine

Identify a white pine by counting its needles— they grow in clusters of five—then see if you can find its monster cones on the ground. The white pine is monoecious, meaning it has both male and female cones on the same tree. The large female cone holds the seeds and lets them out once they're fertilized.

Pinus strobus >

Wild turkey

Gobble, gobble—look for these ground-feeders foraging insects and plants in the brush. Where would you expect a bird this big to sleep? If you are here at dusk, you might get lucky and see the turkeys flying up into the trees where they roost at night. Would you want to sleep in a tall tree all night?

Meleagris gallopavo (in Latin, *gallo* means "chicken" and *pavo* means "peacock") ∧

Wolf tree

Wolf trees are old and overgrown with gnarly limbs. They weren't cut down for pasture with the rest of the forest, so when a new forest grew back, they were bigger than their neighbors. Early foresters saw the old trees as wolfy predators, stealing resources like water and light from prettier, more useful trees. Foresters used to chop wolf trees down, but today they value them as homes for wildlife.

< Keep an eye out for this monster

Seasonal special: Joe Pye weed

These butterfly magnets are tall in summer—you'll walk through a tunnel of them in the first meadow, hopefully when their pink flowers are blooming. Legend has it an American Indian herbalist named Joe Pye made medicine from the flowers that could cure illness. Can you think of any other plants that help people?

< *Eutrochium purpureum*

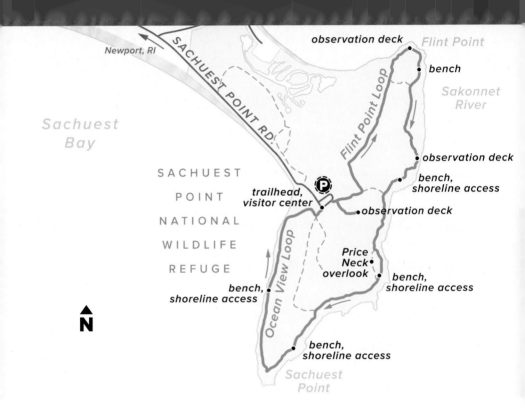

Map labels:
- observation deck — Flint Point
- Newport, RI
- SACHUEST POINT RD.
- bench
- Sakonnet River
- Flint Point Loop
- Sachuest Bay
- observation deck
- SACHUEST POINT NATIONAL WILDLIFE REFUGE
- trailhead, visitor center
- bench, shoreline access
- observation deck
- Ocean View Loop
- Price Neck overlook
- bench, shoreline access
- bench, shoreline access
- bench, shoreline access
- Sachuest Point
- N

YOUR ADVENTURE

Adventurers, each year over 200 bird species swoop through this historic homeland of the Pauquunaukit on the Atlantic Flyway—a highway in the sky. Bring your binoculars to spot as many as you can. Start by getting a lay of the land at the first wooden viewpoint, then head clockwise through the tunnel of shrubs along the Flint Point View Loop and power up on the wooden observation deck. After, head to the shoreline by the bench to

LENGTH

2.6-mile

loop

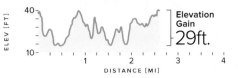

ELEV [FT]

40

10

Elevation
Gain
29ft.

1   2   3   4

DISTANCE [MI]

HIKE + EXPLORE 1.5 hours

DIFFICULTY Easy—mostly flat with a gravel path

SEASON Year-round. Bird-watching is best from April to October and seal-sighting is best in winter.

GET THERE Take 138A / Purgatory Road east of Newport, continue onto Paradise Avenue, and take a slight right onto Hanging Rock Road. Keep right to stay on Sachuest Point Road and follow it to the parking lot at the end.

Google Maps: bit.ly/timbersachuest

RESTROOMS At visitor center

FEE None

TREAT YOURSELF Dare yourself to try an Awful Awful at Newport Creamery, just 4 miles west off Bellevue Avenue—They also have ice cream, burgers, and more goodies with window service.

Sachuest Point National Wildlife Refuge
(401) 619-2680
Facebook @RInwrc

Climb up one of several viewing decks and look out as far as you can

explore the water. Come back to the trail and head to the next observation deck, another bench, and shoreline access. Soon you'll come upon rock outcroppings that are part of the Price Neck Formation, which formed 200 million years ago when the supercontinent Pangaea split—they are pieces of Africa! Climb on top and count the different bird species you see. A little farther along, you'll reach Sachuest Point. Can you spot Newport? The lighthouse at Sakonnet Point? As you continue the loop back to the trailhead, imagine how the land looked when it was covered with farms. Can you picture it during World War II when it was used as a rifle range? At the visitor center, be sure to write any bird species you spotted on the whiteboard.

SCAVENGER HUNT

Seasonal special: harlequin duck

Look for these colorful ducks between October and April on the rocks offshore. See if you can find a male dancing to impress a female. Once a pair forms, they journey together along the Atlantic Flyway to breed and raise their ducklings in warmer southern waters. Mated pairs will often stay together for years.

< *Histrionicus histrionicus* (*histrio* means "actor" in Latin and refers to the ducks' showstopping feathers)

White-tailed deer tracks

This is the only species of deer in Rhode Island—look carefully on the ground for its tracks as you hike. Use your animal detective skills if you spy some: How many deer were there? Which direction were they going? You're most likely to spot the actual deer at dawn and dusk.

Look in the mud for telltale tracks from *Odocoileus virginianus* >

Song sparrow

Look for the song sparrow's brown and white stripes in the branches as you hike. You might hear one before you see it, but keep an eye out, and maybe you'll catch a male singing on an exposed perch. Use your phone's audio app to record the song and replay it later so you can learn to recognize it.

< *Melospiza melodia*

Porcelain berry

These Easter egg–colored berries from the grape family appear in late summer, following small, upright yellow flowers. Imported from Asia in the 1870s for its beauty, this plant is now considered invasive because it crowds out or smothers native plants. It spreads quickly because birds just love the berries, eating them then pooping out the seeds far and wide.

< *Ampelopsis brevipedunculata*
(in Greek, *ampelopsis* means "vine")

Harbor seal

Winter is a great time to catch Rhode Island's official state mammals lounging on rocks like happy bananas. Keep an eye out for pups; they might be hanging out alone on shore or swimming along the edge, waiting for mom to come back with food. Give any seals you see plenty of space so

you don't scare them. Find a spot to do your best seal-banana impression.

Phoca vitulina ⤴

ADVENTURES IN
MASSACHUSETTS

Adventurers, it's time to explore the Commonwealth (another word for state) of Massachusetts. Colonized in 1620 by pilgrims who landed in what is now Plymouth, its name comes from the Algonquian language and means "large hill place." You will definitely see some hills here, shaped and carved by the Laurentide Ice Sheet as it retreated thousands of years ago. Today over 60 percent of Massachusetts is covered in forest. You'll start your adventures on an island, then explore some of the Bay State's 192 miles of coastline as you bird-watch on Cape Cod. You'll head toward the capital, Boston, then roam on geologic drumlins, walk in the footsteps of famous authors, see an old rock grotto and boardwalk, crawl through a chasm, summit a mountain, and count hawks, before making your way west to more mountainous terrain, where you'll bag a rocky peak and find an old plane wreck. Feel the freedom of the state motto as you hike: "By the sword we seek peace, but peace only under liberty." Let's go!

GO SHELLING AT CEDAR TREE NECK SANCTUARY

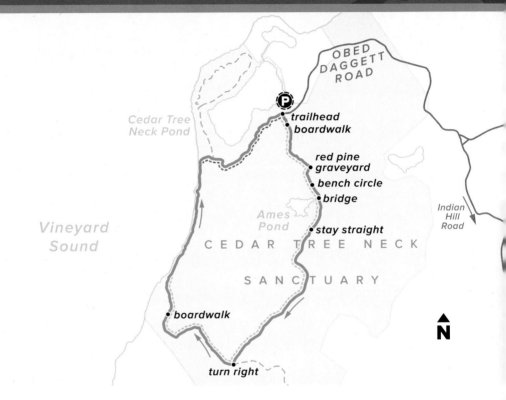

Cedar Tree Neck Pond

OBED DAGGETT ROAD

• **trailhead**
• **boardwalk**

• **red pine graveyard**
• **bench circle**
• **bridge**

Ames Pond

• **stay straight**

Indian Hill Road

Vineyard Sound

C E D A R   T R E E   N E C K

S A N C T U A R Y

• **boardwalk**

• **turn right**

▲
N

YOUR ADVENTURE

Adventurers, welcome to Martha's Vineyard, the historic homeland of
the Wampanoag. This island was partially created from a glacial moraine,
essentially a pile of rocks and sediment left behind as a glacier melted.
Climb up to your left on the white trail—you'll want to keep on the white
trail all the way to the beach, so check the map as you move along to be sure
you're staying on track. Cross a boardwalk, pass the purple trail, and check

LENGTH

1.4-mile

loop

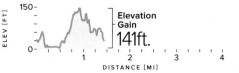

Elevation Gain **141ft.**

HIKE + EXPLORE 2 hours

DIFFICULTY Moderate—some downhill, uphill, and overgrown terrain; you'll need to pay attention to the map

SEASON Year-round. Fall colors are incredible. Be sure to check for ticks.

GET THERE The Steamship Authority ferry from Woods Hole on Cape Cod is the only one that transports vehicles—be sure to make a reservation. Several other passenger-only ferries leave from other destinations. Once on-island, take State Road to Indian Hill Road and go north for 1.3 miles. Turn right onto Obed Daggett Road at the hilltop and follow signs to the end of the road and the sanctuary's parking area.

Google Maps: bit.ly/timbercedartree

RESTROOMS At parking lot in summer and fall

FEE None

TREAT YOURSELF Grab a cookie or brownie (gluten-free and vegan options too) at the Scottish Bakehouse on your way back to Vineyard Haven.

Sheriff's Meadow Foundation
(508) 693-5207
Facebook @SheriffsMeadow

Vineyard Sound crashes on the shoreline for the last part of the hike

out the red pine graveyard. Power up at the bench circle and pass the yellow trail that goes around Ames Pond. Stay straight, passing the blue-yellow trail on your right, approaching Ames Pond and crossing over a brook. Pass the blue-orange trail on your left, continuing straight. At the orange junction, hang a right on white to make your way to the beach. Cross a boardwalk and walk until you see a side trail down to the beach. Walk along the rocky shore, notice the ledge above you, and find as many shells as you can. Soon you'll reach a trail on your right—cross over a boardwalk, take a left, and follow the red trail back to the trailhead.

SCAVENGER HUNT

Cedar Tree Neck Pond

If it's not too windy, close your eyes and listen. How many sounds can you hear? Seagulls? Maybe some chirping frogs? You're standing between two thriving aquatic ecosystems—the freshwater pond and the salty ocean. How do you think life is different in one versus the other? Sketch the view of the pond in your journal.

∧ Power up and take in the view of the pond

Atlantic surf clam

It's another bivalve! Can you tell the difference between this one and a scallop? Challenge a fellow hiker to the Clam Challenge—gather as many clam shells as you can in a minute; no points for other shells. Who got the most? Like all clams, these are filter feeders. They like to bury themselves in the sand so waves don't push them around as they feed.

Spisula solidissima shell >

Atlantic horseshoe crab

More related to spiders than to crabs, these "living fossils" are 200 million years *older* than dinosaurs. Their blood is amazing—it's copper-based, which makes it blue instead of red like our iron-based blood, and it has special properties that help doctors and scientists develop safe medical procedures. Unfortunately, horseshoe crabs are becoming endangered, so if you see a live one, treat it with extra respect.

∧ *Limulus polyphemus*

Atlantic bay scallop

This shell belonged to a bivalve and was one of a pair. Can you guess what bivalve means? As you find shells, compare differences in their size, shape, and color. Scallop shells typically have long grooves on one side, and the joined halves are hinged like a book. A strong muscle opens and closes the halves (this is the part humans and other animals like to eat).

Argopecten irradians shell ⊐

Channeled whelk

This shell belongs to a gastropod, a group of animals that includes all snails—unlike bivalves, their shells are a single piece. Whelks are a predatory snail. Each circle in their cone-shaped shell is called a whorl. If the whorls are knobby instead of smooth, you have found the cousin *Busycon carica*, or knobbed whelk.

< *Busycotypus canaliculatus* is named for the grooves on its shell (in Latin, *canaliculatus* means "with small channels")

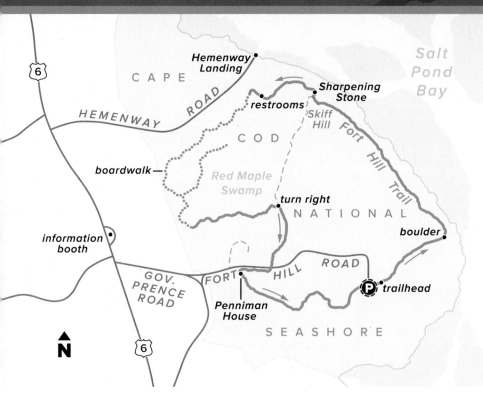

YOUR ADVENTURE

Adventurers, it's time to explore the Nauset Marsh, which opens to the Atlantic Ocean. You're on the Cape Cod peninsula, historic homeland of the Nauset, and the work of that same famous glacier that did all the sculpting around here. Start at the far parking lot on Fort Hill Road and head north along Nauset Marsh, powering up at a couple viewpoints as you pass old

LENGTH

1.6-mile

loop

ELEV [FT]

75—

0—

Elevation
Gain
51ft.

DISTANCE [MI]

HIKE + EXPLORE 1 hour

DIFFICULTY Easy—a nice, flat, wide path

SEASON Year-round. Late spring and early fall are less crowded with no fee.

GET THERE From Orleans on Highway 6, turn right onto Governor Prence Road. After half a mile turn right onto Fort Hill Road and follow to the parking lot at the end.

Google Maps: bit.ly/timberforthill

RESTROOMS Open late spring to early fall at Hemenway Landing about halfway around the loop

FEE None

TREAT YOURSELF Don't leave the Cape without visiting the Local Scoop, a few minutes south in Orleans—try a Cape Cod Pop.

Cape Cod National Seashore

(508) 255-3421 | Facebook @CapeCodNPS

Take in the views of the Atlantic Ocean on a bench at the trailhead.

farmlands to your left—imagine corn and hay growing here in the past. Reach the forest and head straight in until you reach Sharpening Stone on your left. Feel the soft ground beneath you—this is a glacial delta, where the glacier deposited a bunch of sand and boulders. Curve left and stop by the restrooms at Hemenway Landing if you need to. Explore the Red Maple Swamp Trail boardwalks, then turn right on Fort Hill Walk. Take the stairs to Fort Hill Road and safely cross to check out the Captain Penniman House. From here, take Fort Hill Trail back to the parking lot.

SCAVENGER HUNT

Penniman House

If you make a reservation, you can tour inside the house and learn more about it. From outside, sketch some of the special architectural details in your journal, including the mansard roof and the cupola up top where the captain could go to view the sea. Next, sketch your dream house. What special details would it have and why?

ʌ This Second Empire Victorian house was built in 1868 for whaling captain Edward Penniman

Chicory

Find this purple flower in summer and fall—look for its fifteen to twenty petal rays with small teeth on the ends. Play Love me? Love me not? by touching each petal instead of plucking them. Sit still for one minute and watch to see if any bees or butterflies visit the flowers too.

Cichorium intybus >

Great blue heron

Look for this wading bird in the marsh during summertime—they can get up to 4 feet tall. Is that shorter or taller than you? Their wingspan can be over 6 feet. Do you know anybody taller than 6 feet? Imagine having wings that long!

< *Ardea herodias*

Red maple

Can you find the three-lobed leaves of the red maple even if they're still green? They only turn red in autumn before falling off. In spring and summer, look for its seeds—winged helicopters or keys, called samaras, designed to fly in the wind and plant new maples far and wide. Have a helicopter race by dropping two from the same height and seeing which flies the farthest.

< Look for *Acer rubrum* along the Red Maple Swamp Trail

Sharpening Stone

Take a moment at this Nauset Indian grinding stone and imagine sharpening your tools here. Find the different scrapes and imagine the tools they were using. The moon-shaped grooves were for harpoon heads to kill whales and the straight ones were for axes. The stone used to be down in the marsh, but the National Park

Service moved it in 1965. What kind of tools did they need to move it?

Twenty tons of history ↴

18

CAN YOU FIND WORLD'S END?

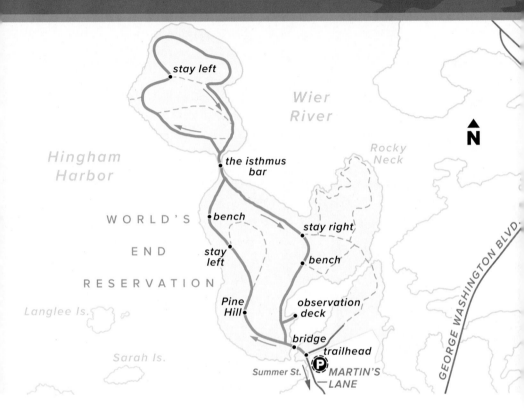

YOUR ADVENTURE

Adventurers, you're hiking the historic homeland of the Massachusett. The small hills in this area are called drumlins and are made of fine-grained sediment left by the receding glacier. They used to be an island at high tide, but colonial farmers dammed the marsh, and now World's End is a peninsula. From the parking lot, cross the first bridge and head left, clockwise around

LENGTH

3.1-mile

figure eight loop

ELEV [FT]

125–

0–

DISTANCE [MI]

1   2   3   4

Elevation
Gain
92ft.

HIKE + EXPLORE 1.5 hours

DIFFICULTY Easy—wide, old carriage paths over rolling hills

SEASON Year-round.

GET THERE From Route 3A, turn onto Summer Street, then left onto Martin's Lane where it intersects with Rockland Street. Follow for 0.7 miles to the entrance and 70-car parking lot.

Google Maps: bit.ly/timberworldsend

RESTROOMS At parking lot

FEE Free for members; nonmembers $10 per car on weekdays, $15 weekends; parking passes are not sold on site—everybody must make a reservation on the website

TREAT YOURSELF Nona's Homemade in Hingham serves cones in flavors like seasonal pumpkin and year-round Hingham Harbor Sludge.

World's End Reservation, The Trustees of Reservations | (781) 740-7233
Facebook @WorldsEndReservation

Hike your way to the
end of the world

the first drumlin, as you climb up Pine Hill. Follow the wide, old road, passing under different kinds of trees—how many varieties can you spot? Power up at a couple benches and pass side trails to your right (stay left). Walk across the isthmus, a strip of land connecting two islands, and power up at another bench before continuing to the left, climbing up drumlin number two. Continue along the perimeter, checking out the view. Stay to your left as you curve around, downhill, and find yourself back at the isthmus. Take one more left to complete your loop, staying straight as you pass side trails to Rocky Neck. There's a final bench before you reach a side trail to a bird observation deck. After checking out the birds, come back to the main trail and end back at the trailhead.

SCAVENGER HUNT

Red fox

Keep an eye on the grassy fields by the trail, and you might spot this mammal darting by. Check out its black "stockings" and bushy tail. Be sure to give it some distance and sketch it in your nature journal.

< *Vulpes vulpes*

Frederick Law Olmsted

In 1890, this famous park planner (NYC's Central Park) designed a housing neighborhood at World's End. The houses were never built, but the carriage paths to serve them still lace the park— imagine horse-drawn carriages clip-clopping along these roads. Would you want to live here? Draw a map and plan your own neighborhood. What would you include or leave out?

The father of American landscape architecture >

Bur oak

Crazy hair day alert! See if you can find this gnarly, wild-capped acorn on the ground August through September—they take a season to grow. Can you guess why this oak is nicknamed mossycup? Find the yellow leaves in fall and trace their round lobes with your finger so you remember their shape even when you can't find the acorns.

< *Quercus macrocarpa*

Isthmus

An isthmus is a thin strip of land with water on both sides connecting two larger landmasses—this one forms a link between the two drumlins you'll hike on today. Be sure to check the tide chart at the start of the trail so when you reach the isthmus you'll know if the tide is high or low.

On the other side, you might be able to see all the way to Boston >

Bird blind

Near the end of your loop, don't miss this spur trail to the bird blind observation deck overlooking Damde Meadows, a tidal marsh that drains at low tide. Look through the slats for herons, egrets, kingfishers, and more. What tide is here now, low or high?

How long can you sit, wait, and watch over the meadow? ∧

19

ROCK OUT AT IPSWICH RIVER WILDLIFE SANCTUARY

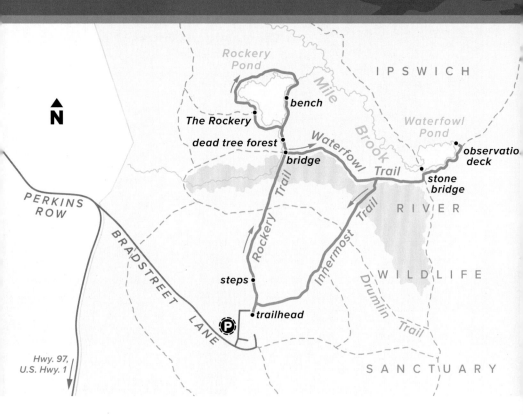

YOUR ADVENTURE

Adventurers, are you ready to explore your first rockery? The awesome rock garden you'll see today is on the historic homeland of the Pawtucket in the Ipswich River watershed. A watershed is an area of land where gravity collects all the water at the lowest point—for the Ipswich River, it's this wetland. You'll start off on the wide and smooth Rockery Trail, heading

LENGTH

1.5-mile

figure eight loop

ELEV [FT] — 125 – 0 –

Elevation Gain

79ft.

DISTANCE [MI]   1   2   3   4

HIKE + EXPLORE 1 hour

DIFFICULTY Easy—fairly flat and short

SEASON Year-round. Beautiful fall colors; peaceful in winter snow; fresh buds and birdsong in spring.

GET THERE From Topsfield, take Perkins Row east until it ends at the parking lot.

Google Maps: bit.ly/timberipswich

RESTROOMS At nature center

FEE $6 nonmember adults, $4 seniors and kids 2–12, free for Mass Audubon members

TREAT YOURSELF Whoopie pies are calling your name—just up the road at Topsfield Bakeshop.

Ipswich River Wildlife Sanctuary,
Mass Audubon Society
(978) 887-9264
Facebook @MassAudubonIpswichRiver

Sit and watch for reflections on Rockery Pond

down some stairs. Cross a bridge and pass through a "tree portal" to another bridge at a fork with the Waterfowl Trail. Head left to the Rockery, a collection of glacial erratic granite boulders that were first dropped all over the region by the retreating ice sheet thousands of years ago, then carted here in 1905 to build this sweet grotto. Wind in and out of the rock city and around Rockery Pond and power up at a bench. Head through a stripped tree forest and pass the bald monster tree, cross the boardwalk, and hang a left on Waterfowl Trail. At a junction, continue straight onto the Waterfowl Trail to the Stone Bridge and bird-watch at Waterfowl Pond. Head back and take a left on the Innermost Trail, passing the Drumlin Trail, on your way back to the parking lot. Be sure to add any bird sightings to the list by the trailhead.

SCAVENGER HUNT

Rockery

It took Italian immigrants with horse-drawn carriages eleven years to cart in all these glacial erratic boulders and arrange them to create the rock garden. How would you move these boulders today? How long might it take?

Thomas Emerson Proctor created an arboretum here and built the Rockery >

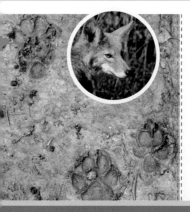

Eastern coyote

Coyotes don't hibernate, so you can find their tracks year-round (winter is especially good because they're easy to see in snow). Can you see how theirs are different from dog prints? They don't usually have claw marks, and the pads are much closer together. What can you tell about an animal from its tracks?

< Look for *Canis latrans* paw prints in mud or snow

Mallard

Stop and watch the pond for at least five minutes—you might see a pair of mallards swim by. The brown females are called hens and the males, with their bright green heads, are called drakes—if you see a group swimming or on the ground, that's called a sord, and if they're flying, it's a flock. Pretend they are leading a game of Simon Says and mimic each new behavior you see.

Anas platyrhynchos ↑

Winterberry holly

These bright red berries do things a little differently than most berries—they like to be out and about in winter. What do you like to do that's different than other people? Is it helpful? Winterberries are a good food source for birds when many other foods aren't available.

< *Ilex verticillata*

American white water lily

Breathe deep if you're here between spring and fall—can you smell the sweet fragrance of these white flowers? Their scent will be strongest in the morning hours, when they first open. Count all the floating pads you can spot. The roots go down, down, down into the mud at the bottom of the pond.

Nymphaea odorata (in Latin, *odorata* means "perfumed") >

20

GET BACK TO NATURE AT WALDEN POND

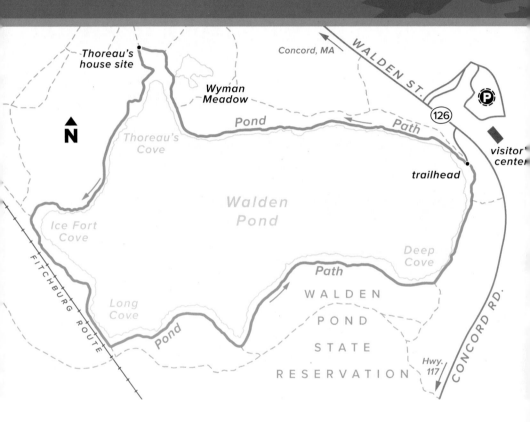

Concord, MA

WALDEN ST.

Thoreau's house site

Wyman Meadow

Pond Path

126

P

N

Thoreau's Cove

visitor center

trailhead

Walden Pond

Ice Fort Cove

Deep Cove

FITCHBURG ROUTE

Path

WALDEN

Long Cove

Pond

POND

STATE

Hwy. 117

CONCORD RD.

RESERVATION

YOUR ADVENTURE

Adventurers, would you want to live by yourself for two years? What would you do all day? Ponder that as you hike to the spot where Henry David Thoreau's one-room house, or hermitage, once stood. He built it himself and lived there from July 1845 to September 1847. Head counterclockwise from the beach—you are walking on top of 450-million-year-old granite in the historic homeland of the Pawtucket. On your right is Wyman Meadow

LENGTH

1.7-mile

loop

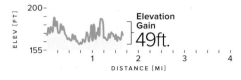

Elevation Gain 49ft.

ELEV [FT] · 200 · 155
DISTANCE [MI]

HIKE + EXPLORE 1 hour

DIFFICULTY Easy—fairly flat and short; no hand-holding spots

SEASON Year-round. Swimming (and crowds) in summer, snow (and peace) in winter.

GET THERE In Concord, turn off Walden Street into the main parking lot, then cross the street at the crosswalk.

Google Maps: bit.ly/timberwalden

RESTROOMS At visitor center

FEE $8 MA residents, $30 nonresidents

TREAT YOURSELF Get a sandwich or some locally famous seasonal pie to go at Verrill Farm just few miles west, off Sudbury Road.

Walden Pond State Reservation, Massachusetts Department of Conservation and Recreation

(978) 369-3254 | Instagram @MassDCR

You'll be circumnavigating this famous pond today

and to the left is Thoreau's Cove—keep an eye out for birds here. Find the site of the original house and power up. Continue along the Pond Path, passing Ice Fort Cove, Long Cove, Little Cove, and Deep Cove—power up at each and contemplate their differences. Ignore side trails on your right and stick to the Pond Path around the water. Be sure to check for ticks after. Do you have a spot that is as special and peaceful to you as Walden Pond was to Thoreau?

SCAVENGER HUNT

White oak

Use a pencil to make a rubbing of an oak leaf in your nature journal, label it, and compare it to a leaf from another tree. What is the same and what is different? Thoreau thought observing and living near nature was valuable. He wrote in his journal, "A river, with its waterfalls and meadows, a lake, a hill, a cliff or individual rocks, a forest, and ancient trees standing singly. Such things are beautiful; they have a high use which dollars and cents never represent. If the inhabitants of a town were wise, they would seek to preserve these things." What do you think?

∧ *Quercus alba*

The hermitage spot

Thoreau's friend and fellow writer Ralph Waldo Emerson let him build a small house on this spot (there's a replica at the visitor center). He lived here in semiseclusion (he had visitors and often visited friends in town) as he wrote his first book. Add a stone to his memorial cairn while thinking about what the woods have taught you and how you would like to live your life.

∧ The house's original site, discovered nearly 100 years after Thoreau left Walden Pond

Walden Pond

In his book *Walden*, Thoreau described the pond as "blue at one time and green at another, even from the same point of view. Lying between the earth and the heavens, it partakes of the color of both." What color would you say it is today? Walden is a kettle pond. Imagine the last glacier melting away, leaving a big ice cube melting in a deep hole

(102 feet deep!), eventually creating the pond. Do the Walden Challenge: sit still and watch the pond for five minutes (set a timer on your phone). Afterward, write in your nature journal about what you saw, felt, and heard.

View of the pond from the beach ⌐

American red squirrel

"All day long the red squirrels came and went, and afforded me much entertainment . . . running over the snow-crust by fits and starts like a leaf blown by the wind . . . suddenly pausing with a ludicrous expression and a gratuitous somerset . . . before you could say Jack Robinson, he would be in the top of a young pitch pine . . . chiding all imaginary spectators, soliloquizing and talking to all the universe at the same time—for no reason that I could ever detect." Today gray squirrels (*Sciurus carolinensis*) are also common around Walden. Besides their color, they are also larger than their red squirrel cousins. Sit quietly and you may see both squirrels gathering food around the pond. Write your own description of what they're up to.

∧ Thoreau described *Tamiasciurus hudsonicus* in *Walden*

21

ROCK HOP THROUGH PURGATORY CHASM

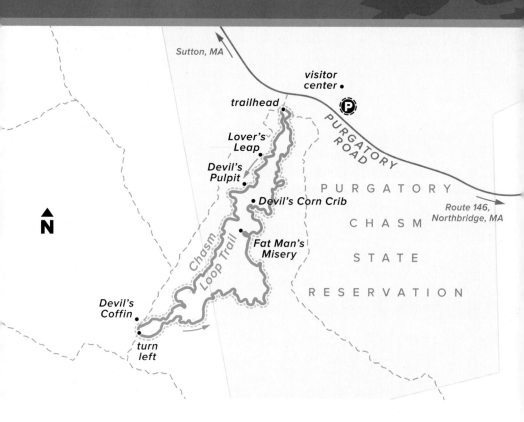

YOUR ADVENTURE

Adventurers, get ready to walk through the bottom of a chasm that's 70 feet deep. Scientists aren't totally sure how this deep fissure formed. The current best guess is that a sudden flood of glacial meltwater flowed through here around 14,000 years ago—the granite walls withstood the flood but

ELEV [FT]

675—

425—

Elevation Gain
94ft.

1   2   3   4

DISTANCE [MI]

LENGTH

0.7-mile loop

HIKE + EXPLORE 1 hour

DIFFICULTY Moderate—nice and short, but negotiating some of the boulders can be difficult for smaller kiddos; the loop return is above the chasm, so you'll want to have them stay close

SEASON Spring through fall; closed in winter.

GET THERE From Route 146, take exit 6 to head west on Purgatory Road. Park near the visitor center on the right.

Google Maps: bit.ly/timberchasm

RESTROOMS At visitor center

FEE From Memorial Day weekend through October 31, $5 for MA residents, $20 for nonresidents

TREAT YOURSELF Just half a mile east on Purgatory Road, West End Creamery has over sixty flavors of ice cream to choose from.

Purgatory Chasm State Reservation, Massachusetts Department of Conservation and Recreation

(508) 234-3733 | Instagram @MassDCR

ᐱ Be sure to wear good clambering shoes for this hike

the rock between them was swept away. You're on the historic homeland of the Nipmuc. Follow blue blazes painted on the granite for half a mile as you wind your way up, down, and around. Keep your eyes peeled for Lover's Leap and Devil's Pulpit on your right. After Devil's Coffin, turn left on Chasm Loop Trail to climb above the chasm—watch little ones here, as you'll be walking along a steep edge. Stop to explore Fat Man's Misery and Devil's Corn Crib before you complete the loop.

SCAVENGER HUNT

Root wedging

See if you can find evidence of tree roots wedging into the rock, spreading and creating long cracks. Trace a root with your finger to see where it goes. One day, these cracks will spread wide enough to cleave the rock into pieces. Is there anything else growing on the rock? What effect do you think these other organisms might have on it?

∧ Roots, roots everywhere

Black birch

Find these oval-shaped, toothed leaves shading the canyon. Feel the tree's smooth bark on its trunk and roots. Early colonists used to tap black birch trees for sap (just like maple trees) and use it to make birch beer. It tastes similar to root beer and you can still buy it today! How old do you think these trees are?

Watch *Betula lenta* light up the chasm in gold each fall >

Fat Man's Misery and Devil's Corn Crib

Explore these deep cracks if you dare. What came first—the rock or the trees around it? What evidence do you have? Unlike other cracks in the park, these probably weren't formed by trees. What do you you think could make cracks this straight and deep in rocks so big?

Can you fit in the crack? ↗

Eastern chipmunk

These squirrel cousins love beechnuts and other berries and seeds. Most of the year, they're out during the day, gathering food in their cheek pouches to take back to underground burrows— multi-chamber systems with rooms for sleeping, storing food, pooping, and having babies. You won't see them in winter because they stay home sleeping, only waking up every couple days to eat and use the bathroom.

∧ *Tamias striatus*

Barred owl

Mass Audubon says this bird's call sounds like "who cooks for you, who cooks for you all?" Listen to a recording so you can recognize it if you hear it. What does it sound like to you? Barred owls are more active during the day than other owl species. Their brown feathers help them blend in against bark, and they can stand very still.

< *Strix varia*

22

HAWK WATCH ATOP MOUNT WATATIC

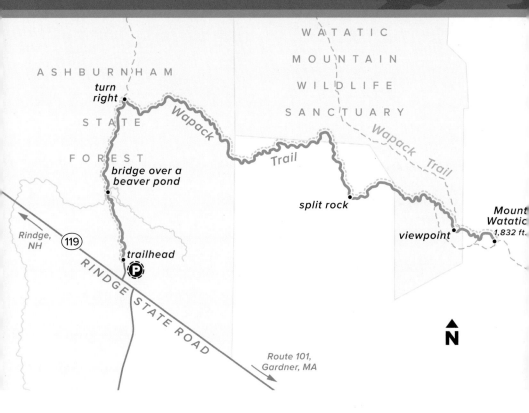

YOUR ADVENTURE

Adventurers, today you're summiting a monadnock, an isolated hill that was more erosion resistant than its surroundings and stood the test of time as the landscape around it was scraped low. You'll start on the historic homeland of the Pennacook in the Wapack Range and follow the yellow blazes of the Wapack Trail. Cross footbridges over a beaver pond and make

LENGTH

2.7 miles

out and back

Elevation Gain
588ft.

ELEV [FT]
1,875–
1125–

DISTANCE [MI]
1   2   3   4

HIKE + EXPLORE 2 hours

DIFFICULTY Challenging—steep ascent with lots of roots, but also fairly short with plenty of power-up spots

SEASON Year-round. Icy and snowy in winter; can get muddy in spring rains; great fall bird-watching.

GET THERE The parking lot is on the north side of Route 119 / Rindge State Road near the state border.

Google Maps: bit.ly/timberwatatic

RESTROOMS At parking lot

FEE None

TREAT YOURSELF Stop by Carol's Ice Cream for hot dogs or a cotton candy sundae, 7 miles northwest on Route 119.

Friends of the Wapack, Willard Brook State Forest (for parking) | (978) 597-8802 Facebook @FriendsoftheWapack

Are you ready to climb this monadnock?

a quick right over a stone agricultural wall to stay on the trail as the elevation starts to pick up. This trail was built in 1923 and is considered one of the first intrastate hiking trails in the region. Cross a small creek, pass through a split boulder, and continue the climb. Stop at a viewpoint to see Mount Wachusett and Little Watatic Mountain. At a small trail junction, turn right to the summit. Walk all around the meadowlike summit and make sure to visit East Watatic, about 100 yards past the first summit. These lookouts are your best chance for views and hawk watching. Retrace your steps and go left to head back to the trailhead.

SCAVENGER HUNT

Beaver

The pond you pass near the beginning of the hike was built by beavers who dammed streams to create a wetland. For a chance at spotting one of these aquatic rodents, sit quietly on a bridge and challenge yourself to watch the water quietly for at least two minutes (set a timer on your phone). This pond is nameless—what name would you give it?

Castor canadensis >

Peregrine falcon

Falcons tend to have more slender wings with pointier tips than their broad-winged hawk cousins. The peregrine falcon is the fastest bird on Earth. It can dive through the air at up to 200 miles per hour in a unique move called a stoop. Do a peregrine race with your hiking buddy—who can stoop the fastest?

Falco peregrinus >

Rocky summit

You're at the southern end of the Wapack mountain range. A ski area operated here until 1984, and a fire tower was open to the public until 1996. The summit almost became the site of a cellphone tower, but the town of Ashby and other conservation groups were able to purchase the land and protect it.

< Look around the rock piles for a commemorative stone

Seasonal special: lowbush blueberry

Once you get up high enough, you'll see lots of low bushes with small oval leaves. In spring, these have white bell-shaped flowers, but summer (July is best) is when the real fun begins—it's blueberry time!

< *Vaccinium angustifolium*

Seasonal special: broad-winged hawk

In fall, join other hawk-watchers helping to count the birds as they migrate. Bring something warm so you can sit comfortably for a bit. Look to the north—that's where they're migrating from. Scan all over the sky instead of just looking in one place. Broad-wings are a smaller hawk, crow-size, with a black-and-white tail. If you're lucky, you'll see a group, called a kettle, swirling in circles.

< *Buteo platypterus* (in Latin, *platy* means "wide" and *pterus* means "wings")

23

DESCEND TO DOANE'S FALLS

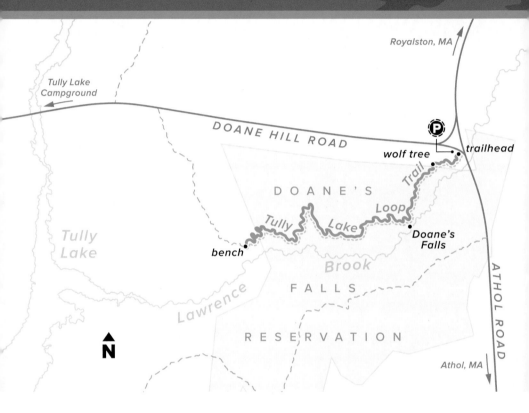

YOUR ADVENTURE

Adventurers, today you'll walk the historic homeland of the Pennacook along Lawrence Brook as it tumbles down to Tully Lake. The 175-foot chain of waterfalls is named for Amos Doane, who built a mill above the falls in the early nineteenth century for making doors and window blinds. Take the blue-blazed trail downstream, stopping at fence-protected viewpoints

ELEV [FT]

875–

625–

Elevation Gain 176ft.

1 2 3
DISTANCE [MI]

∧ Take in the rush of the falls while you power up

LENGTH

1 mile out and back

HIKE + EXPLORE 1 hour

DIFFICULTY Moderate—short with a minor descent/ascent; watch little ones near edges

SEASON Year-round. Best spring through fall; winter can be very icy.

GET THERE Just south of Royalston on Athol Road, turn right on Doane Hill Road to find the parking lot.

Google Maps: bit.ly/timberdoanes

RESTROOMS Down the road at Tully Lake Campground

FEE None

TREAT YOURSELF Roadside homemade ice cream and foot-long hot dogs await at Lickity Splitz in Winchendon, off Route 202.

The Trustees of Reservations
in season: (978) 249-4957
off season: (413) 684-0148
Facebook @TheTrustees

along the way. Follow the cabled fence, being careful with littles near the edge. Look for the first observation point on the left; here you can see the top of the falls near the stone bridge on Athol Road. Keep going and see if you can find all four small falls before you reach the flat area with a bench near the 20-foot lower falls. Check out the rock that the falls tumble over. It's metamorphic, which means it has been changed by heat and pressure. How is it different from other rock you've seen in Massachusetts? When you're done, head back the way you came and consider camping at Tully Lake Campground just down the road.

SCAVENGER HUNT

Tribute to Edward Franklin Bragg

Take a look at this engraved mill-stone memorial for Edward Bragg, a descendant of the Doanes. He was hoping to use water in the river for a hydroelectric dam. How might the land around here have changed if he was successful?

< August 28, 1863–June 2, 1923

Leaf miner

Look closely at the leaves along the trail. Do you spy with your little eye any white, winding trails? Certain kinds of fly, moth, and beetle larvae munch on leaf tissue and leave this wiggly evidence. Draw a leaf-tunnel maze in your nature journal for someone to solve.

The very hungry larva >

Eastern hemlock

This evergreen conifer guides your way down the trail. Look closely at its tiny cones—find one that's about to open and keep it in a paper bag at home until the seeds come out. Notice how hemlock needles grow in a flat plane along their stem—this is a good way to tell hemlocks apart from similar conifers like fir trees, whose needles stick out in every direction, making each stem look bushy. Does your hair look more like needles from hemlock or fir?

< Tsuga canadensis

Paper birch

Can you guess how this tree got its name? Keep an eye on the ground, and you'll find plenty of the papery bark to experiment with. Use a sharp stick to draw a picture on the bark's white side or collect some pieces to use as kindling for your campfire. Birch bark makes an excellent fire starter because it stays dry even if everything else in the forest is wet. This waterproofness also makes it excellent for building canoes.

< Betula papyrifera

24

CLIMB GOAT PEAK TOWER AT MOUNT TOM

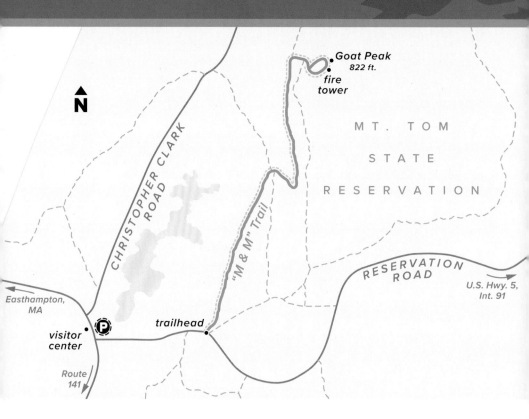

YOUR ADVENTURE

Adventurers, you're on the historic homeland of the Nipmuc in an area they call Norwottuck, meaning "in the middle of the river." You'll be climbing an old fire tower to look for hawks and views. These hills are part of the Mount Tom Range and are capped with basalt, an igneous rock that used to be lava. Imagine 200 million years ago, when dinosaurs roamed and the valley

ELEV [FT]
1,000 –
500 –

Elevation Gain 300ft.

DISTANCE [MI]
1   2   3   4

Climb the tower and look for Mt. Monadnock to the north and Hartford, Connecticut, to the south

LENGTH

1.2 miles out and back

HIKE + EXPLORE 1.5 hours

DIFFICULTY Moderate—short, but with steep, rooty sections

SEASON Year-round. Hawk migration and great foliage in fall; the access road is plowed during winter, but take precautions on snowy, icy trails.

GET THERE North of Holyoke on Route 141, turn right on Christopher Clark Road for 2.3 miles. The visitor center and parking lot will be on the left.

Google Maps: bit.ly/timbergoat

RESTROOMS At parking lot near the visitor center

FEE $5 MA residents, $20 nonresidents

TREAT YOURSELF Small Oven Bakery, just 5 miles west on Union Street in Easthampton, is waiting for you with delicious sandwiches or croissants to go for your power-up stops.

Mount Tom State Reservation, Massachusetts Department of Conservation and Recreation (413) 534-1186 | Instagram @MassDCR

below you was filled with lava—pretend the dirt is lava and rock hop as far as you can. From the parking lot, walk briefly on the side of Reservation Road until you see the Metacomet-Monadnock trailhead on your left. Follow the white blazes of the "M&M" Trail up, up, up, passing a maple grove and a bench for power-ups. Climb the final push up to the tower then up its steps for a view and a chance to spot some hawks. Count the tower steps on your way down and thank your legs for having carried you up each one. Carefully hike back to the parking lot the way you came.

SCAVENGER HUNT

Goat Peak Tower

Built in 1912 and staffed 24/7, the original fire tower on this spot was struck by lightning and destroyed in 1924. It was rebuilt as this 30-foot metal tower in 1928. Can you imagine spotting fires from up here? What else can you see from this viewpoint?

Up the steps you go >

Shelf mushrooms

These mushrooms are polypores, which means they hold their spores in tubes and decompose wood. Notice how the underside is more textured than the topside—it's covered in tiny holes, the ends of the tubes holding the spores that make new mushrooms. These mushrooms are important because as they break down dead wood, they return nutrients to the soil for other plants to use. How many fans can you find on one log?

∧ Fan-shaped *Trametes elegans* grow on logs and stumps

Seasonal special: red-tailed hawk

In fall, particularly in September, use binoculars to look for this buteo hawk from the top of Goat Peak's tower. Look for its wide red tail and listen for its screechy call as it soars on thermals (currents of warm air in the sky). Sketch its outline in your nature journal. Remember its call and listen for it when you watch TV later—shows often use the sound to represent any hawk or eagle.

< *Buteo jamaicensis*

Funnel web grass spider

Look in the grass for these spiders' sheetlike webs with a funnel on one end. Unlike other spiders, these don't spin sticky traps. Instead, they hide in the funnel until they sense a bug walking across the web—then they dart out to catch it. They are super fast! Their bites aren't harmful to humans, but you could easily harm them. If you see one, respectfully keep your distance.

< *Agelenopsis* species

Sweetfern

Find some of these leaves on the ground and crush them to release their sweet smell. Despite its common name, this plant is not actually a fern but a shrub. What are some things that make it different from a true fern?

Comptonia peregrina >

25

PICNIC LIKE AN AUTHOR ON PEESKAWSO PEAK

YOUR ADVENTURE

Adventurers, you're on the historic homeland of the Mohican. From the trailhead, take the yellow-blazed Hickey Trail to the right to start. Soon, take a left to begin your ascent. You'll pass a big flat rock perfect for a power-up before a series of rock stairs. Pass a cave on your left and cross a bridge over a stream, and soon you'll come to Inscription Rock, which

LENGTH

2.8-mile

loop

1,800–

ELEV [FT]

800–

Elevation Gain

664ft.

1   2   3   4

DISTANCE [MI]

HIKE + EXPLORE 2 hours

DIFFICULTY Challenging—steep ascent and an unprotected summit

SEASON Year-round. Beautiful fall colors; fun winter snowshoeing.

GET THERE The parking lot is off the west side of Route 7 / Stockbridge Road, north of Great Barrington.

Google Maps: bit.ly/timbermonument

RESTROOMS At parking lot

FEE Free for Trustees members; $5 for nonmembers at a machine that takes cards in the parking lot

TREAT YOURSELF After summiting, grab an oatmeal pecan cookie or chocolate croissant at Berkshire Mountain Bakery, just 5 minutes away, off Route 183 / Park Street.

The Trustees of Reservations, West Region
(413) 200-7262
Facebook @West.Region.90

From the summit, the Berkshire Mountains reach out as far as the eye can see

commemorates the land. Power up here for the final push. Head up the red trail, tackling the rocky steps to the peak—watch little ones on the edges and keep in mind these lines from William Cullen Bryant's 1815 poem about the mountain: "The beauty and the majesty of earth, / Spread wide beneath, shall make thee to forget / The steep and toilsome way." He's saying the view from the top is worth the work. What do you think? On the way back, head left at Inscription Rock on the blue Mohican Monument Trail, a gentle downhill that curves to the road. Turn left at the bottom and follow the road back to the start.

SCAVENGER HUNT

Herman Melville and Nathaniel Hawthorne Cave
In August 1850, the two authors went for a hike here. A thunderstorm forced them to hole up in a cave like this one, and they talked all night about ideas that Melville would eventually include in his book, *Moby Dick*. Take a minute to talk with your hiking buddy about ideas for your own Great American Novel.

< Deep cover for deep thoughts

Striped maple
These trees are also called moosewood and goosefoot. Can you guess why? In winter, when there's not much to eat, moose eat its bark. Look for the deciduous leaves from spring through fall—some people think they

look like goose feet. How would you walk with feet like that?

Acer pensylvanicum: goose or moose? ◄

Pin oak

This tree has leaves with sharp, widely spaced lobes, and it makes acorns in autumn. They start out green and eventually turn brown. Arrange some acorns in a pattern and let your hiking buddy study it for 30 seconds. Then cover their eyes, and remove one acorn. Can they figure out which is missing?

< *Quercus palustris* leaves and acorns

American chestnut

These were once the most common trees in New England, sometimes growing up to 200 feet tall. Then a blight (a type of fungus) killed them off. Today, you can find some young trees scattered through the forest, but the blight will kill them before they get very old. Find one of the toothy leaves on the ground and bring it home. Press the shape into some aluminum foil and use that to make a foil press stamp.

Castanea dentata (in Latin, *dentata* means "toothed") ⌐

Quartzite

This pale rock is metamorphic quartzite—super-old beach sand that transformed under intense squishing pressure and heat. Half a billion years ago, Africa collided with North America, pushing up the Berkshire Mountains and uncovering this rock. Quartzite is tough and hard to erode, which is why it sticks around in cool shapes as surrounding rock gets carved away. Clank two pieces together—what do you notice?

∧ This metamorphic rock makes up the mountain you're climbing

26

FIND THE WRECK AT ROUNDS ROCK

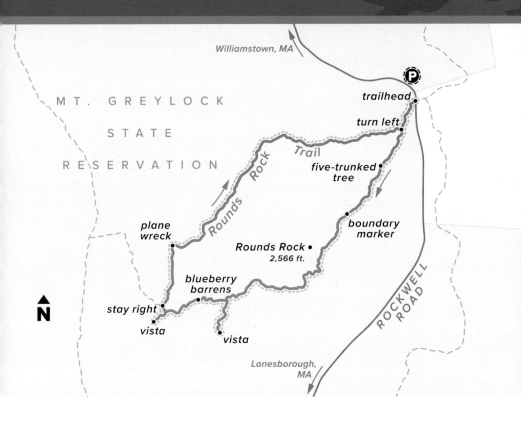

Williamstown, MA

MT. GREYLOCK STATE RESERVATION

trailhead

turn left

Rounds Rock Trail

five-trunked tree

plane wreck

boundary marker

Rounds Rock •
2,566 ft.

blueberry barrens

stay right •
vista

• vista

ROCKWELL ROAD

Lanesborough, MA

N

YOUR ADVENTURE

Adventurers, this is a short but sweet loop near Massachusetts's highest point, Mount Greylock, on the historic homeland of the Mohican. Start off at the trailhead across the road from the day-use parking—be sure you see the sign for Rounds Rock. This well-marked, blue-blazed trail is named for farmer Jabez Rounds. Head left at the first fork to start your loop. Walk by

ELEV [FT]

2,875–

Elevation Gain
110ft.

2,425–

DISTANCE [MI]

1   2   3   4

LENGTH **0.7-mile** loop

HIKE + EXPLORE 1.5 hours

DIFFICULTY Easy—nice and short with very little elevation gain; a few rocky parts, so be sure to hold younger hands at viewpoints

SEASON Gate open late May through October; blueberries in summer and colors in fall.

GET THERE From Route 7 in Lanesborough, head north on North Main Street, turn right on Greylock Road, then left on Rockwell Road. After 3.5 miles, park on the right side of the road in the day-use spots.

Google Maps: bit.ly/timberrounds

RESTROOMS Down the road at the Mount Greylock State Reservation Visitor Center

FEE $5 MA residents, $20 nonresidents

TREAT YOURSELF The Store at Five Corners has pumpkin bread, huge cookies, and full-service dinner with pasta and sandwiches, just a few miles north on Highway 7.

Mount Greylock State Reservation
(413) 499-4262
Instagram @MassDCR

∧ Take in one of two great viewpoints

the five-trunked tree and a granite slab marking the boundary between the towns of New Ashford and Cheshire. Soon you'll approach a left turn for your first vista. Walk safely to the ledge—it's made from a metamorphic rock called schist that appears layered thanks to its transformation under heat and pressure—power up and take in the view. Head back to the main trail and turn left, passing a rocky barren (a flat area with poor soil where only certain plants can grow) with blueberry bushes. Find a sign indicating a vista and an airplane wreck. Head left for the vista, crossing over a few rocky surfaces (careful if wet) and power up if you need. Return to the main trail and follow the sign to the wreck. Investigate the plane's remains and read about the pilot. Complete the loop by turning left to head back to the trailhead. When you're done, consider camping at Mount Greylock Campground nearby.

SCAVENGER HUNT

Seasonal special: white meadowsweet
Find these spikes of white flowers drinking in the sun during summer. Look closely, with a hand lens if you have one. Can you count five petals? How many stamens, the pollen-carrying threads, can you count popping out of each one? American Indians use meadowsweet's toothy, lance-shaped leaves to make tea.

Spiraea alba >

Tawny grisette mushroom
During summer, look closely for this gilled mushroom, the fruiting body of a fungus. As it grows, its cap changes from a ball to an umbrella to a flat plate. How do people look different as they grow? How old do you think the mushroom you found today is?

Amanita fulva >

Plane wreck

The remnants of this twin-engine Cessna create a memorial for John Newcomb, a retired World War II pilot who crashed here while delivering newspapers in 1948 during a foggy and rainy night. Pilots nicknamed these kinds of planes "bamboo bombers" because they were made mainly of wood.

Find the wreck and memorial toward the end of the hike >

Red-spotted purple admiral butterfly

From May to September, keep your eyes peeled in the forest for this black-and-blue beauty. It uses mimicry to disguise itself as a swallowtail butterfly, which predators don't eat because they know they're poisonous. Mimic a fellow hiker by talking and walking just like them (but only for a minute or two!).

< *Limenitis arthemis*

Red spruce cones

Merry Christmas! These festive-looking evergreen conifers keep their leaves (needles are just special leaves) year-round and grow their seeds inside cones. Look for their cones in fall—are the scales open or closed? What do you think this means? Crush some needles and take a whiff—what do you smell?

Can you find *Picea rubens* cones? ↗

ADVENTURES IN
VERMONT

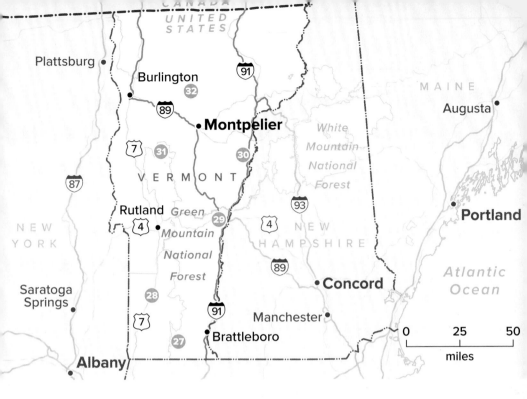

Welcome to the Green Mountain State, adventurers. French explorer Samuel de Champlain called this region Verd Mont, or "green mountain," and it became a state in 1791. Vermont's Green Mountains are the northernmost portion of the Appalachian Mountain Range. They're made of granite and stretch the length of the state. The same Connecticut River you explored way down in Connecticut forms the border between Vermont and New Hampshire—its 406 miles start near New Hampshire's border with Quebec. At 4395 feet, Mount Mansfield is Vermont's highest point—maybe one day you'll climb it. Until then, you can still get plenty of views. You'll scale rocky peaks and ledges, climb a fire tower, walk down a massive gorge, and visit waterfalls. Look for evidence of old farms in the woods. In the nineteenth century, people cut down trees for farming, stacking rocks to make walls. By the twentieth century, many had moved to cities or other states. The trees grew back, but the walls and building foundations stayed. As you travel, channel the state motto—"Freedom and Unity"—with each step.

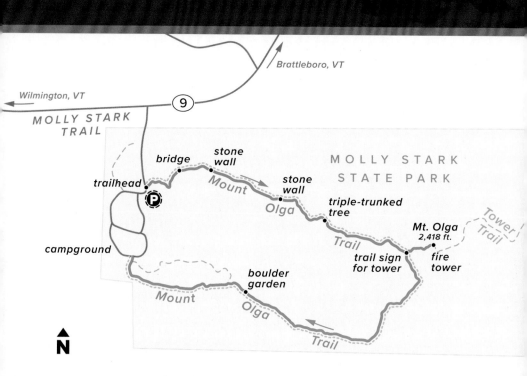

YOUR ADVENTURE

Adventurers, the state park that's home to Mount Olga sits on the historic homeland of the Abenaki and is named for the wife of Revolutionary War general John Stark. She was a nurse who became famous thanks to her husband's battle cry urging his troops to victory: "They are ours, or this night Molly Stark sleeps a widow!" You'll start out going clockwise, taking

LENGTH

2-mile

loop

ELEV [FT]

2,550–

1,800–

Elevation Gain

521ft.

DISTANCE [MI]

1 2 3 4

HIKE + EXPLORE 1.5 hours

DIFFICULTY Moderate—short, but rocky and rooty in some parts; gentle elevation gain

SEASON Year-round. The gate is closed November to April but that just adds a short walk on pavement.

GET THERE East of Wilmington on VT-9, turn south into the Molly Stark State Park parking lot.

Google Maps: bit.ly/timberolga

RESTROOMS At parking lot

FEE None

TREAT YOURSELF Hogback Mountain Country Store has maple creemees and cider donuts with a view waiting for you just a couple miles east.

Molly Stark State Park | (802) 464-5460
Facebook @VTStateParks

How many peaks can you see from the top of the tower?

the trailhead closest to the highway and following the blue blazes. Cross a bridge over the creek and begin gently climbing, passing two old stone walls. Soon you'll see the tower peeking through the foliage—climb your way up, up, up. How many stairs can you count? Once you reach the top, how many peaks can you see in the distance? After descending the tower, head back and complete the loop (be sure you take the rest of the loop down and don't continue past the tower), passing a boulder garden and walking back to your car in the parking lot. Make a weekend of it and camp at one of the park's lovely campsites.

SCAVENGER HUNT

Yellow birch forest

In fall, walk through this yellow canopy on your way down. Yellow birch bark is shiny, and its leaves are oval with serrated edges—if you find a twig on the ground, break it in two and take a whiff for a fresh wintergreen-like scent.

Betula alleghaniensis >

Fisher

This carnivorous (meat-eating) weasel is sometimes called a fisher cat, but it isn't a cat and it doesn't fish—its name comes from *fichet*, a French word for a similar-looking European polecat. Fishers are shy, so you're unlikely to see one on the trail, but keep a keen eye out for their dens in tree cavities—they have their babies, called kits, in March.

< Pekania pennanti

Fire tower

Mount Olga is named for Wilmington resident Olga Haslund, who gifted these 48 acres to the state in 1939. The fire tower was moved here from Bald Mountain in 1945, and firefighters used it as a lookout until the 1970s. Power up and look for peaks from the cab on top. Look east for Vermont's Green Mountains and New Hampshire's Mount Monadnock. Can you spot the Berkshire Mountains to the south? What state are they in?

< Are you ready to climb?

Seasonal special: trout lily

These lance-shaped leaves are mottled (another word for speckled) like the backs of brook trout underwater. You'll find them in spring along with, for a few early weeks, yellow flowers that nod down. These flowers love sunlight. They close up at night and won't open if the day is cloudy. Can you relate? The leaves last longer than the flowers, but they also disappear by summer.

Erythronium americanum ↗

Many-trunked red maple

Red maples sometimes sprout from a stump; it's likely that this tree fell or was cut down, then several sprouts grew from the stump so that now the trunks grow in a ring. Give a high five to each trunk and place a gift, like a pine cone or colorful leaf, in the center to thank the tree for helping make clean air for you to breathe.

< *Acer rubrum*

GO WILD AT LYE BROOK FALLS

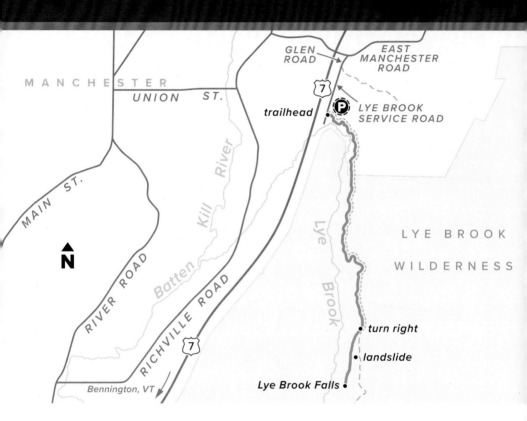

GLEN ROAD

EAST MANCHESTER ROAD

MANCHESTER

UNION ST.

7

trailhead

P

LYE BROOK SERVICE ROAD

Batten

Kill

River

River

MAIN ST.

RIVER ROAD

N

Lye

Brook

LYE BROOK

WILDERNESS

RICHVILLE ROAD

7

turn right

landslide

Lye Brook Falls

Bennington, VT

YOUR ADVENTURE

Adventurers, get ready because today we're visiting the historic homeland
of the Mohican to feel the mist from one of Vermont's highest waterfalls.
Sign the hiker register box and note how many adventurers have come
before you. Enter Lye Brook Wilderness and stay left as you begin this
blue-blazed roller-coaster climb on the Lye Brook Trail. Stop to power up

^ Relax at Lye Brook Falls

ELEV [FT]

1,700-

700-

DISTANCE [MI]

1 2 3 4

Elevation Gain
853ft.

LENGTH

4.6 miles out and back

HIKE + EXPLORE 2 hours

DIFFICULTY Challenging—one of our longest hikes, with high elevation and rocky terrain, but more than doable with power-up stops; watch littles near steep edges

SEASON Year-round. Fall is gorgeous and dry with fewer bugs; spring brings mud and black flies; winter is icy and the road is not plowed.

GET THERE From Highway 7, take VT-30 east and turn right on East Manchester Road. Go south on Glen Road / Lye Brook Falls Service Road for half a mile to the parking lot at the end.

Google Maps: bit.ly/timberlyebrook

RESTROOMS None

FEE None

TREAT YOURSELF Mother Myrick's Confectionery on Main Street Manchester has loads of fun candy.

Green Mountain and Finger Lakes National Forest, Manchester Ranger Station

(802) 362-2307

Facebook @GreenMountainFingerLakesNF

often, listening to the brook that runs along the trail the whole way—this is one of our longer adventures. In 1912, the Rich Lumber Company ran a 16-mile-long railroad that brought logs from these woods down to a mill in Manchester. Can you imagine a railroad running up this hill? Cross a few streams and head under a few downed tree arches as the trail gradually heads up. Finally, you'll reach a junction with the Lye Brook Falls Trail to the right—take that a little bit downhill and be careful to watch littles or hold hands at the exposed edge. Cross an area that had a landslide in 2011 during Tropical Storm Irene, then arrive at beautiful 125-foot Lye Brook Falls. Be careful on the slippery rocks. Power up and soak in the details at the falls before carefully heading back the way you came.

SCAVENGER HUNT

Lye Brook Wilderness sign

Welcome to the wilderness, a protected area where human activities are limited. In the 1700s, there used to be two different mills, owned by the Burritt Brothers and Pettibone Brothers, that drew power from Lye Brook, but today the creek and over 18,000 acres around it are free from any human development. Close your eyes and appreciate the sounds of nature uninterrupted.

Look for this sign that marks the entrance >

The Dalton Formation

Geologists call a series of similar rocks "formations"—these blocky chunks of quartzite are a part of the Dalton Formation. Pick up a piece and describe what you see when you look closely. Why do you think it breaks into blocks the way it does?

Look for this crumbly gray quartzite >

Paper birch

Look for this tree's dangly catkins in April and May. If any are on the ground, put them by your ears and take a catkin-earring selfie. See if you can find some white bark on the ground—it peels off as the tree grows and really feels like paper. Use a piece to make a card for your hiking buddy.

< *Betula papyrifera* catkins

Seasonal special: great white trillium

Look for the proud, tall white flowers in spring and early summer—even

before they bloom, their triangular whorls of three leaves are noticeable. Look closely under the flower—there are three skinny green bracts in a beautiful pattern—take a moment to sketch what you see from a bird's-eye view, then kneel on the ground to sketch from another angle. What is different?

< *Trillium grandiflorum* (can you guess how this plant got its name?)

Seasonal special: Dutchman's breeches

Another white flower you might catch in early spring, these distinctive blooms inspire so many different images (hearts, underwear)—rename them for something you think they look like. Flowers like this are able to grow in early spring because the trees above them don't have leaves yet. Once the forest floor gets shady, different plants will grow.

Dicentra cucullaria (in Latin, *cucullio* means "hood") >

YOUR ADVENTURE

Adventurers, you're on the historic homeland of the Abenaki. You'll be hiking down, up, and back again in Vermont's Little Grand Canyon—it's 165 feet deep and a mile long. From the visitor center, head out the back and start your descent on the wide, flat trail. You'll come out to the main trail right near the Quechee Gorge Bridge and come upon the Ottauquechee

LENGTH

2-mile

T-shaped out and back

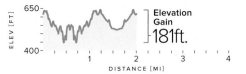

ELEV [FT]

650

400

Elevation Gain
181ft.

1 2 3 4

DISTANCE [MI]

HIKE + EXPLORE 1 hour

DIFFICULTY Easy—light elevation gain for big reward; watch littles near the ledge

SEASON Year-round. A good hike for muddy springs as the trail has gravel packing it down.

GET THERE Just south of Hartford on Highway 4, the visitor center and parking lot are on the south side of the road before the bridge.

Google Maps: bit.ly/timberquechee

RESTROOMS At visitor center

FEE None

TREAT YOURSELF Get some crepes at the Skinny Pancake, just to the west on Highway 4.

Quechee Gorge State Park
(802) 295-2990
Facebook @VTStateParks

The rocks at the bottom of the gorge are a great place for play

("swiftly moving water" in Abenaki) River. Power up at the bench and turn left to head all the way down into the gorge. Walk out on the rocks and check out the view of the bridge. Head back up the trail, pass your power-up bench, and continue to follow the main trail until you pass under the bridge. Keep walking along the road until you reach the falls created by a dam that was built to power an old wool mill operated by A. G. Dewey from 1869 to 1962. Head back the way you came and consider spending the night at the campground.

SCAVENGER HUNT

Quechee Gorge Bridge

People have long needed a way to get across Quechee Gorge. The first bridge here was made from wood in 1875. This bridge replaced it in 1911 and is Vermont's oldest standing steel bridge today. Look closely at its truss pattern (those triangles supporting each other). Gather some sticks and create your own truss structure. How much weight can it hold?

285 feet long ↗

American robin

The robin's red chest is easy to spot, especially in spring when it comes back from wintering in the south. Listen for their cheery-sounding repeating chirps. Robins are omnivores—their diet is mostly berries, but they are famous for catching worms. Watch one quietly and you might see it pounce ferociously on its lunch.

< *Turdus migratorius*

Mill Pond Falls and Dewey Mills Dam

This dam was originally built over the 41.4-mile-long Ottauquechee River to power the Dewey Woolen Mill. Today it's a hydroelectric facility run by Green Mountain Power. How do you think a dam generates power?

The Ottauquechee River lives up to its name, even with a dam >

Metamorphic rocks and glacier evidence

Look for your reflection in the pools at the bottom of the gorge—imagine these rocks under miles of ice. Thousands of years ago, a huge glacial lake started to drain, releasing tons of water and gradually carving the gorge. Look for the east-dipping layers that look like they're sliding sideways into the Earth. What do you think could cause this?

< Metamorphic rocks are formed from heat and pressure

Monarch butterfly

As caterpillars, monarchs eat milkweed, which is poisonous to many other creatures. As grown butterflies, they are toxic to predators, and their bright colors let everyone know it. Each year before winter, the butterflies migrate to Mexico. Volunteers for the Vermont Institute of Natural Science net and tag them to observe their patterns and learn about them. Share your own sightings at journeynorth.org.

∧ *Danaus plexippus*

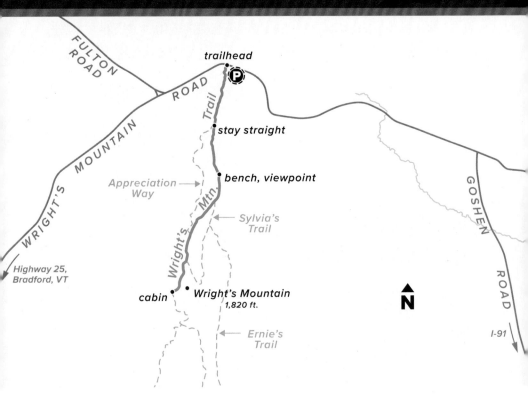

YOUR ADVENTURE

Adventurers, let's grab ourselves a great view of the 24.5-mile-long Waits River Valley on the historic homeland of the Abenaki and rest in a sweet cabin, shall we? Begin your journey by signing the trail log—read some other visitors' entries for fun. This trail was designated a National Recreation Trail in 2018 as part of the 50th anniversary celebration of the

LENGTH

1.8 miles

out and back

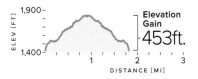

ELEV [FT]

1,900–

1,400–

Elevation Gain

453ft.

DISTANCE [MI]

1 2 3

HIKE + EXPLORE 1 hour

DIFFICULTY Easy—light elevation gain for big reward; watch littles near the ledge

SEASON Year-round. Great fall colors; be cautious during winter snow.

GET THERE Take Goshen Road north of Bradford. Turn left on Wright's Mountain Road. After 1 mile, the parking lot will be on your left.

Google Maps: bit.ly/timberwrights

RESTROOMS A couple hundred y... the trail on the left

FEE None

TREAT YOURSELF Red Kite Cand... Bradford has fresh caramels.

Upper Valley Land Trust
(603) 643-6626
Facebook @UpperValleyLandTrus...

The cabin at the summit

National Trail System. The mountain is named after an early Bradford settler, Benoni Wright, who tried to do a religious fast (no eating) for forty days in a cave nearby. Head straight up on this unblazed but well-signed trail—it's a former logging road, so it is wide and fairly level. Pass the yellow-blazed Appreciation Way on your right and Sylvia's Trail on your left as you stay straight along the way. Halfway up, there's a bench at a viewpoint that's perfect for a power-up. What can you see down in the valley? Look for 4802-foot-tall Mount Moosilauke across the state border in New Hampshire before continuing onward to the cabin and lookout. Take in the views and head back the way you came.

SCAVENGER HUNT

The Gile Mountain Formation

Wright's Mountain is part of the 400-million-year-old Gile Mountain Formation. This metamorphic rock is made from oceanic mud and clay that was squeezed and changed when Africa collided with North America. Collect a few pieces and examine closely—are the grains big or small? Shiny or dull?

A piece of ancient muddy ocean floor >

Ruffed grouse

This bird has amazing wings. If you startle it from a hiding spot, it will explode up and away with a loud wing clap. In spring, males attract females by drumming—rotating their wings back and forth so quickly they create a mini sonic boom! In winter, ruffed grouse grow special bristles on their toes that act like snowshoes to help them walk better.

∧ *Bonasa umbellus*

North American porcupine

These quilled rodents are mostly active at night, but you could get lucky and spot one at dusk. Keep an eye on the hemlock trees, because porcupines snack on their twigs. If you visit in winter, you might find their tracks—they kind of look like small, close, bear tracks with long toes. Can you or your hiking buddy guess how many quills one porcupine can have? Almost 30,000!

Erethizon dorsatum (in Latin, this name means "animal with the irritating back") ∧

Pileated woodpecker

Knock, knock. Who's there? Woodpecker. Woodpecker who? Listen for this red-headed bird tapping away on a nearby tree—up to 12,000 times per day! What is something you do 12,000 times a day? A year? Look for the rectangular holes it makes in rotting trees or logs while on the hunt for insects like ants.

< *Dryocopus pileatus* (in Latin, *pileatus* means "capped")

Cabin

From the cabin window, look for 3144-foot Mount Ascutney and the Green Mountains in the far distance. Landowners Ernie and Sylvia Appleton loved this mountain and built the cabin in the 1960s so they could spend more time here. It had glass windows, a door, and a wood-burning stove with a brick chimney. If you were to build a cabin, where would it be and what would it look like? Draw it in your nature journal.

Come on in! ↗

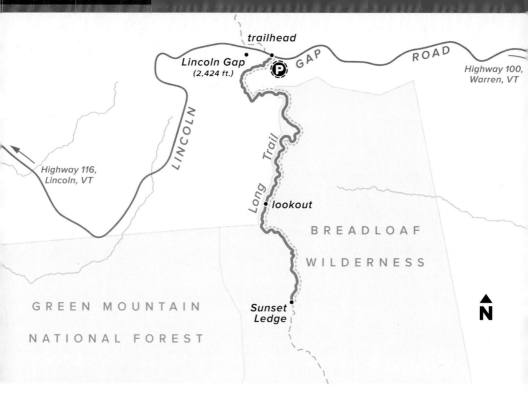

YOUR ADVENTURE

Adventurers, we're on the historic homeland of the Abenaki, and we're here for the view. We'll be climbing a ridge between Mount Grant and Lincoln Gap, but it's over so quick you'll barely feel the elevation gain. Follow the white blazes of the Long Trail and register your party at the Breadloaf Wilderness stand. At 25,000 acres, this area is about the size of Disney World.

LENGTH

1.5 miles

out and back

Elevation Gain

343ft.

ELEV [FT]
2,900
2,400

DISTANCE [MI]
1   2   3   4

HIKE + EXPLORE 1.5 hours

DIFFICULTY Moderate—quick and scrambly elevation gain to a flat ridge; watch littles at the top

SEASON Lincoln Gap Road is closed from late fall to spring depending on the season: be sure to call and check. Fall is great for colors and fewer bugs.

GET THERE From VT-100, head west on Lincoln Gap Road for 4 miles. The trailhead will be on your left.

Google Maps: bit.ly/timbersunset

RESTROOMS None

FEE None

TREAT YOURSELF Grab a maple with sprinkles at the Village Creeme, 10 miles west in Bristol.

Green Mountain National Forest
(802) 747-6700
Facebook @GreenMountainFingerLakesNF

The view from the ledge

After a switchback, keep your eyes peeled for white blazes to start appearing on rocks on the right-hand side of the trail. Climb up the rock (watch your littles) and get back on the dirt trail. Soon you'll reach the ridgeline, where, finally, the trees will open up to a view from Sunset Ledge. Touch the wavy-looking rock under your feet here—this metamorphic schist is part of the Green Mountains, a 250-mile-long section of the Appalachian Mountain Range that's been around for a billion years, eroding slowly over time. Power up for a billion nanoseconds (one full second) or more and return the way you came.

SCAVENGER HUNT

Long Trail blaze

Built by the Green Mountain Club between 1910 and 1930, the Long Trail, at 272 miles (before counting side trails), is the oldest long-distance hiking trail in the United States. What is the most days you think you could hike in a row? Two days? Five? The average time to hike the whole Long Trail is twenty days.

A short bit of the Long Trail >

Hobblebush

This shrub is called hobblebush because of how it spreads low on the ground, hobbling anyone who tries to walk through it. Spot the heart-shaped leaves year-round and white flowers in springtime. In winter, its brown buds look like moose ears so some people call it "moosebush." What name would you give it based on some part of the way it looks today?

< *Viburnum lantanoides*

Black bear

Bears love Breadloaf Wilderness, but they're quite shy—be sure to make noise as you hike, to give them a chance to hide. If you come upon one, back away and maintain eye contact, but don't run. You're more likely to see a bear's scat (poop) or the scratch marks it left on a tree where it stopped to eat a fruity snack.

Ursus americanus >

Seasonal special: purple trillium

This plant grows on the forest floor in spring, before the trees overhead get their leaves. Look for its three leaves, three petals, and three sepals (special leaves under the petals that protected the flower bud before it bloomed). What would it look like with six leaves, six petals, and six sepals? Sketch whichever you think you'd like best.

< Trillium erectum (in Latin, *tri-* means "three")

Black-capped chickadee

Look for this little songbird's round body and black cap as it perches sideways or even upside down to feed. Try to whistle its song if you hear it—just two notes, the second lower than the first. These birds don't migrate, so you can find them year-round.

< Poecile atricapillus

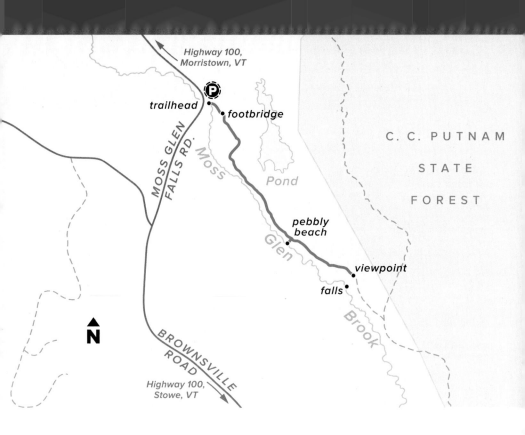

YOUR ADVENTURE

Adventurers, we're on the historic homelands of the Abenaki. You'll start off with a walk along the footbridges with the 5.25-mile-long Moss Glen Brook on your right and a small pond on your left. When you reach a forested spot, the rocky river will reveal the base of the 125-foot falls. The water here is

ELEV [FT]

1,000–

Elevation Gain
]100ft.

750–

DISTANCE [MI]

1   2   3   4

∧ Moss Glen Brook has
a long way to fall

LENGTH

0.5 miles out and back

HIKE + EXPLORE 1.5 hours

DIFFICULTY Easy—short and sweet and sometimes wet, but boardwalks keep it from getting muddy

SEASON Year-round. Best in summer and fall for the colors.

GET THERE From Stowe, take VT-100 northeast and turn right onto Randolph Road. Half a mile later, turn right onto Moss Glen Falls Road. The parking lot will be on your left.

Google Maps: bit.ly/timbermoss

RESTROOMS None

FEE None

TREAT YOURSELF Snag a classic hot cider and cider donut at Cold Hollow Cider Mill, 10 miles south on VT-100.

C. C. Putnam State Forest, Vermont
Department of Forests, Parks, and Recreation
(802) 476-0170
Facebook @VTStateParks

funneled through a ravine made of Stowe Formation schist until it tumbles over a drop, creating the falls. Imagine the power of the moving water—it was once harnessed to run a sawmill nearby. Power yourself up with the view and some lunch, then head back the way you came.

SCAVENGER HUNT

Seasonal special: swamp aster

This flower loves wet soil, so you'll find it near the brook and pond as you walk over the boardwalks. It blooms in late summer— if you find one, count how many petals it has. Be careful with the stems, because they are covered in prickly hairs.

Symphyotrichum puniceum >

Stowe Formation

Any time you see a waterfall, it means the water has met something that's harder to erode away than the rest of the stream or riverbed. In this case, it's the metamorphic Stowe Formation, made from schist, green-stone, and amphibolite—these all started the rock cycle as sediment, like sand or mud, before heat and pressure changed them into the rocks you see today. Look closely and see if you can tell the different kinds of rock apart.

Metamorphic rock lines the gorge >

Beaver dam

Beavers have chisel-shaped teeth that never stop growing, which makes them perfect for chewing on wood. How long do you think it took one to get this far on the tree? They use waterways for travel, cover, even refrigeration. If an area doesn't have as much water as they like, they will engineer the land to create their own pond. Look at this pond—what would you need to do to shape it the way you want it?

∧ Can you spot the signs of beavers?

Peregrine falcon

Look closely at the cliffs next to the falls—you might spot these superfast birds of prey nesting in fall before they migrate south. Their nests, called eyries or aeries (*air*-ees), are exciting to see, because, not long ago, peregrine falcons were almost extinct. A chemical called DDT was making their eggs so fragile that when mom or dad sat on the nest, the eggs would break. The government banned DDT in 1973, and conservation groups have helped the birds get off the endangered species list.

Falco peregrinus >

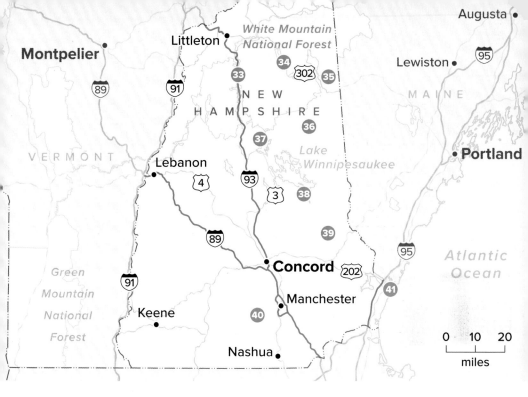

Adventurers, it's time to explore the Granite State—
and it won't take much driving to reveal how it got its nickname. Starting in
the north, you'll cut through the White Mountains and pass by the highest
point in the state, 6288-foot-tall Mount Washington (which maybe you'll
summit one day!), to explore a glacial gorge, four waterfalls, and a kettle
pond. In the New England Upland, you'll summit a mountain, climb one of
the state's sixteen historic fire towers, find the bottom of a chasm, and end
in the Coastal Lowlands, where you'll find WWII landmarks and walk out to
the very tip of the state. Driving up through the capital of Concord along
some of the most scenic highways on the planet, you'll pass through notches,
the valleys dug out by the same glacier you've been following throughout
New England. Over 80 percent of New Hampshire is forested, and should
you visit in fall you'll see what seems like 80 percent of all colors. This was
the first state to declare its independence from Great Britain in 1776—shout
the state motto, "Live Free or Die," as you hike its corridors. Let's go!

33

FLY THROUGH FLUME GORGE

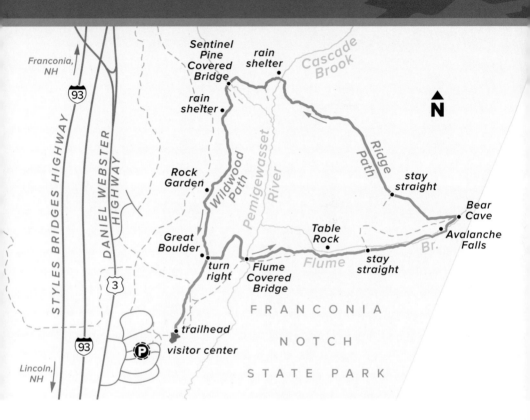

Franconia, NH

93

STYLES BRIDGES HIGHWAY

DANIEL WEBSTER HIGHWAY

Sentinel Pine Covered Bridge

rain shelter

Cascade Brook

N

rain shelter

Wildwood Path

Pemigewasset River

Ridge Path

stay straight

Bear Cave

Rock Garden

Great Boulder

turn right

Flume Covered Bridge

Table Rock

Flume

Avalanche Falls

Br.

stay straight

3

93

Lincoln, NH

trailhead

visitor center

P

F R A N C O N I A

N O T C H

S T A T E   P A R K

YOUR ADVENTURE

Adventurers, you're in the Franconia Range. Check out the peaks as you hike on the historic homeland of the Abenaki. Start on the gravel outside the visitor center, pass a glacial boulder, and turn right for the Flume. Walk through the covered bridge and power up at the huge cascade known as Table Rock. Next, it's time to climb the boardwalk of the Flume itself.

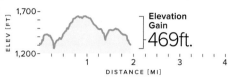

ELEV [FT]

1,700–

1,200–

Elevation
Gain
469ft.

1   2   3   4

DISTANCE [MI]

Are you ready
to rock the
boardwalk?

LENGTH

1.9-mile loop

HIKE + EXPLORE 1.5 hours

DIFFICULTY Easy—nice, short, and easy,
with a boardwalk and wide paths

SEASON May through October (dates may
vary with weather; be sure to check).

GET THERE From Lincoln, take Highway 93
north to exit 34A to reach the visitor center.

Google Maps: bit.ly/timberflume

RESTROOMS At visitor center

FEE $16 adults, $14 kids 6–12, free for kids
under 5

TREAT YOURSELF Ice Cream Delights in
Lincoln scoops Gifford's hardpack and soft
serve (cash only).

Franconia Notch State Park
(603) 745-8391
Instagram @NHStateParks
Facebook @NewHampshireStateParks

Walk up to Avalanche Falls and Bear Cave, then cross Flume Brook. Stay straight on the Ridge Path until you pass over Cascade Brook, power up at a rain shelter, and cross Sentinel Pine Covered Bridge over the Pemigewasset River. Right after, climb down into Wolf Den to cool off and come back up to head down the Wildwood Path toward the Rock Garden. You'll reach the Great Boulder once again—stay to the right here to make your way back to the start.

SCAVENGER HUNT

Table Rock

This gigantic cascade is made from Conway granite—a special type of granite that has been used to build important monuments and once made up New Hampshire's famous Old Man of the Mountain. Smoothed by Flume Brook, Table Rock is 500 feet long and 75 feet wide. How many years do you think it took to get this smooth?

< Have you ever seen rock this smooth?

Avalanche Falls

Check out the Conway granite the river has exposed—it's really hard and resistant to erosion, so the water wore away other kinds of rock first, carving out the gorge. When a homesteader named Aunt Jess Guernsey first discovered the gorge, a huge boulder was stuck, hovering over where the stairs are now. Visitors had to duck under it to see the gorge until 1883, when storm flooding washed it away. The boulder has never been found. Where do you think it went?

45 feet of falls >

Sentinel Pine Covered Bridge

Look down from this kissing bridge at the Pemigewasset River ("swift, side-entering current" in Abenaki) that rolls for 65 miles. Imagine a 90-foot pine tree, the Sentinel, watching over the pool then falling in a 1938 hurricane. Workers laid the tree's trunk over the river then used other trees that fell in the storm to build the covered bridge. Instead of nails, they used wooden pegs to hold everything together. Gather some twigs and construct your own mini-bridge—what do bridges need to work?

Time to cross this 60-foot-long bridge built in 1939 ⏷

Wolf Den

This portion of Conway granite created a "den." Look at how the den is put together—what forces do you think helped create it? Feel its walls and imagine 200 million years ago when they were molten magma. Does that make the rocks igneous, metamorphic, or sedimentary? If taller adventurers don't want to go through the cave, they can walk around the outside and meet you at the end ladder.

You'll climb up these stairs at the end of the den ⏷

Seasonal special: Jack-in-the-pulpit

Find this unique flower March through June. Look closely at its spathe, the special leaf that acts like a protective "pulpit" where "Jack," the stem covered in tiny flowers (called a spadix), stands. In fall, Jack is covered in bright red berries and the spathe withers away to show him off better.

< *Arisaema triphyllum*

34

ROCK STEP TO ARETHUSA FALLS

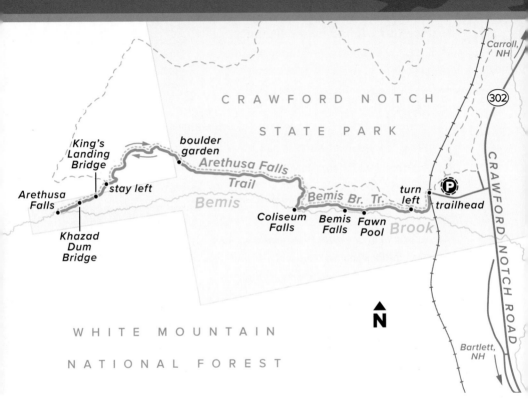

YOUR ADVENTURE

Adventurers, today you get to see not one, not two, not three, but *four* water-falls on the historic homeland of the Abenaki. Keep this reward in mind because you'll need to climb a bit to get there. Cross the train tracks in the second parking lot and start your ascent through the Crawford Notch forest, following the blue blazes. Soon, you'll reach a fork—turn left on the

LENGTH

2.8 miles

out and back

Elevation Gain

849ft.

HIKE + EXPLORE 2 hours

DIFFICULTY Challenging—steady uphill, rocky and rooty; be careful of littles while climbing up from Bemis Brook

SEASON Year-round. Ice tracks or snow-shoes recommended in winter; spring has best water flow, and fall has lovely colors.

GET THERE Just off Highway 302 in Crawford Notch State Park, turn west onto Arethusa Falls Road. Drive up to the second parking lot if you can.

Google Maps: bit.ly/timberarethusa

RESTROOMS At first parking lot

FEE Optional $5 cash donation

TREAT YOURSELF Grab some Gifford's Ice cream at Willey House, just up the road.

Crawford Notch State Park
(603) 374-2272
Instagram @NHStateParks
Facebook @NewHampshireStateParks

Coliseum Falls tumbles down ancient steps

yellow-blazed Bemis Brook Trail that runs alongside the babbling, 2.5-mile-long Bemis Brook. After stopping off at Fawn Pool, Bemis Brook Falls, and Coliseum Falls, look up the hillside—you'll need to make your way back up to the main trail via a root ladder. Scramble up the roots (be careful) and look out for the yellow blazes all the while until you see the sign for Arethusa Falls. Give a tree a hug to thank its roots for help, then make your way up the many stone and log steps. You'll cross the King's Landing Bridge (named for both *Game of Thrones* and Bill King, the man who lives at the trailhead)—do your best royal pose. Head up again and cross the last bridge, Khazad Dum (named for *Lord of the Rings*), before heading down, down, down to where spectacular Arethusa Falls tumbles in front of you. Power up here and come back the way you came. Consider camping at Dry River Campground.

SCAVENGER HUNT

Coliseum Falls

Thanks to their shape, these falls are named for the famous Roman amphitheater. Give a short performance for any frogs that might be watching. Sketch the falls in your nature journal and count the tumbles they do on the rocks.

< These 25-foot falls rush into a small gorge

Seasonal special: pink lady's slipper

From May to June, look for this delicate pink bloom, also called a moccasin flower. This orchid is New Hampshire's state wildflower, common in New England woods, but almost impossible to grow anyplace else because it has a special relationship with a fungus that's only found here. Draw a character in your nature journal with flowers for feet and give it a name.

Cypripedium acaule >

Bemis Brook and Falls

Samuel Bemis, a dentist from Boston, bought this land in 1841 and took this picture with one of the first daguerreotype cameras sold in this country, which put the image on a copper plate. He's buried nearby at the Notchland Inn, his former granite mansion.

Take a picture today and pretend you're Dr. Bemis capturing the landscape. How has photography changed since his day?

< One of the first landscape photographs *ever*; The 10-foot falls today ⬈

Arethusa Falls

At almost 200 feet high, this is the highest waterfall in New Hampshire. It is named after the mythic Greek nymph Arethusa, who transformed herself into a freshwater fountain. Make up a story about what happens next to Arethusa as you explore the falls dropping over this pink Osceola granite.

< How might this view be different in winter or spring?

Tree cave

Think of the effects of wind and rain on this trail. What forces do you think caused this tree to topple over? Does it still seem healthy? Look closely for evidence that shows what role it plays in the forest community today.

Time to take shelter >

35

MOONWALK ON BLACK CAP MOUNTAIN

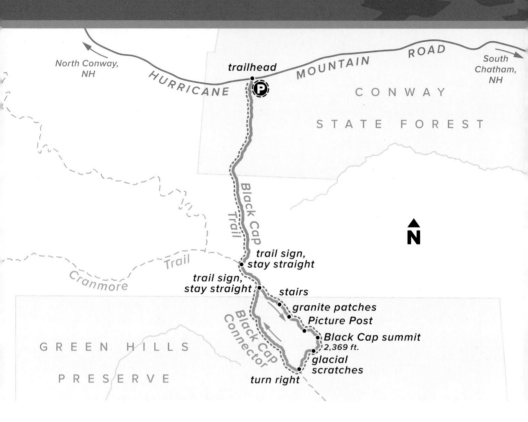

North Conway, NH

HURRICANE

trailhead

MOUNTAIN ROAD

South Chatham, NH

C O N W A Y

S T A T E   F O R E S T

Black Cap Trail

N

Trail

Cranmore

trail sign, stay straight

trail sign, stay straight

stairs

granite patches

Picture Post

Black Cap Connector

Black Cap summit 2,369 ft.

glacial scratches

G R E E N   H I L L S

P R E S E R V E

turn right

YOUR ADVENTURE

Adventurers, you're about to explore a special peak on the historic home-land of the Abenaki. Be sure to sign your name in the register and see all the other fun places people have come from to enjoy this trail. Begin with a gradual ascent among the trees—when you reach a junction, keep going straight up, but remember the turn because that's the way you'll come down

LENGTH

2.3-mile

lollipop loop

2,400—

ELEV [FT]

1,650—

Elevation Gain

634ft.

DISTANCE [MI]

1   2   3   4

HIKE + EXPLORE 1.5 hours

DIFFICULTY Moderate—short but rocky steps; slab hiking at the end (though summit is protected)

SEASON Spring through fall. Hurricane Mountain Road is closed in winter.

GET THERE From North Conway, head east on Kearsarge Road for 1.5 miles, then turn right on Hurricane Mountain Road for 2.6 miles until the parking lot on the right.

Google Maps: bit.ly/timberblackcap

RESTROOMS None

FEE None

TREAT YOURSELF Zeb's General Store in North Conway is full of yummy goodies that are perfect to pack for the top of Black Cap.

Green Hills Preserve,
The Nature Conservancy
(603) 224-5853
Facebook @TNCNH

This rocky, surface-of-the-moon summit has great views of the White Mountains on this lollipop loop. As you walk over granite patches, be sure to look for red blazes on the rock. Soon you'll reach the summit and a memorial rock. Take in the view and keep walking until you reach a path that curves back around to the right. Go straight through the next couple junctions until you find yourself back at the first junction, which is the trail that leads downhill back to your car.

SCAVENGER HUNT

Glacial polish and scratches

Check out these scratches (striations) on the Conway granite (see page 196). Most of the rock is smooth because the receding glacier polished it like fine-grained sandpaper would, but some bigger rocks in the underside of the glacier created these deep scratches. Have you ever polished something smooth? What tools did you use?

Glacial polish on granite >

European pine sawfly caterpillar

Not all caterpillars turn into butterflies—this is the larva stage of an invasive species of sawfly. They lay their eggs in pine needles and drop as larvae to the ground in early summer. You'll be batting them away as flies in autumn.

< *Neodiprion sertifer*

Scat

It's poop time! Always have your poop goggles on—they can help you understand which animals have been in the area and what they've been up to. To figure out who left the scat, look closely for signs of what it ate. Do you see any berries, seeds, or grass?

What do you think left this? >

Red spruce

Take a deep breath at the summit and smell these evergreen conifers (cone-producing) baking in the sun. If you find a branch on the ground, save its shiny needles and the scales from its cone in a baggie. When you get home, stick the pieces in a fun pattern to the back of some tape to make yourself a spruce bracelet.

< Picea rubens

Picture Post

Want to be a citizen scientist? Help the Nature Conservancy monitor the forest throughout the seasons—set your phone or camera on the post and take a picture of the Green Hills. You can submit your photo to the website listed and high-five your hiking buddy for helping conservation efforts.

< There are two interactive stations on your route

ROAM AROUND WHITE LAKE

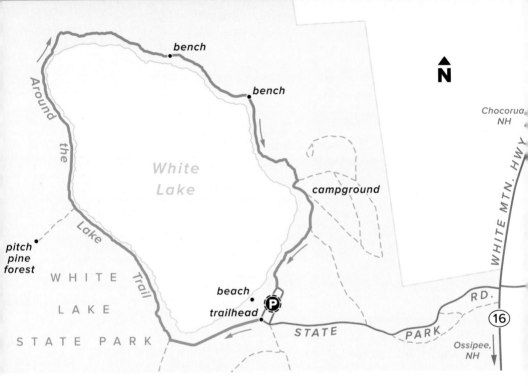

bench

bench

Chocorua, NH

Around

the

White Lake

Lake

pitch pine forest

WHITE

LAKE

Trail

beach

trailhead

STATE PARK

campground

STATE   PARK

RD.

WHITE MTN. HWY

16

Ossipee, NH

N

YOUR ADVENTURE

Adventurers, today you'll be circling this kettle pond on the historic homeland of the Abenaki. It formed after the receding glacier left a chunk of ice behind to melt, creating a hole with fresh water in it. Start off on the beach and turn left on the Around the Lake Trail, walking past the pitch pine forest

LENGTH

2-mile

loop

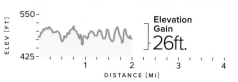

Elevation Gain
26ft.

HIKE + EXPLORE 1.5 hours

DIFFICULTY Easy—nice and flat

SEASON Year-round. Staffed May through October; great summer swimming.

GET THERE Park entrance is on the west side of NH-16 in Tamworth. Park by the beach. Trail starts on the left if facing the lake.

Google Maps: bit.ly/timberwhite

RESTROOMS At parking lot

FEE $5 adults, $2 kids 6–11

TREAT YOURSELF Don't miss the famous pancakes and award-winning maple syrup at Rosie's Restaurant, just up the road.

White Lake State Park
(603) 323-7350
Instagram @NHStateParks
Facebook @NewHampshireStateParks

Can you spot Mt. Chocorua and the Sandwich Mountains?

on your left. As you cross the footbridges, keep an eye out for loons and other birds on the lake. Curve around the north end and power up at any of the benches as you make your way back to the beach. Stick around to camp after.

SCAVENGER HUNT

Wintergreen

These leaves stay mostly green year-round but sometimes turn red in cold weather. Crush one in your hand and inhale the scent—the flavor is popular for gum and toothpaste. Technically, wintergreen isn't a kind of mint (it's more closely related to cranberries). Next time you're in the checkout aisle, see if you can find some mislabeled wintergreen "mints."

Gaultheria procumbens (in Latin, *procumbens* means "lying facedown") >

Pitch pines and red pines

The pitch pines on the left-hand side of the trail are some of the oldest in the state, but they can be hard to tell apart from their cousins the red pines. Both have flaky, puzzle-piece bark and cones with pointy scales that have sap in them. Both have needles that grow in a bundle, or fascicle, but a pitch pine's needles grow in threes and a red pine's grow in twos. These trees are resilient and fire-resistant. Are you resilient? How do you react after something difficult?

∧ *Pinus rigida* (pitch) or *Pinus resinosa* (red)?

Loon calls

Look for the black-and-white checks of the loon in summer and their gray-and-white fall color. Listen for its eerie call. "Oooooo-OOOOOOOOOOOO," almost like a sad wolf saying, "I'm here!" Practice making the call yourself—if you get good enough, they'll answer you back.

Gavia immer (in Swedish, *immer* means "dark ashes") >

Honey mushroom

Who is your best friend? Do you have one, two, ten? Look for gilled honey mushrooms in a friendly cluster coming out of wood or on the ground. Link your arms with all the other hikers in your group to make your own honey mushroom cluster.

Armillaria mellea >

Black cherry

Look for these shiny leaves with a pointed tip—if you find one on the ground, crush the leaf to smell its cherry fragrance and maybe put on some cherry perfume or cologne. In summer, the red berries turn black—birds love them. Other parts, like the bark, can be toxic to wildlife, but are used in small amounts in human medicine. Have you ever had wild cherry cough syrup? The flavor is extracted from this bark.

< *Prunus serotina*

37

SUMMIT WEST RATTLESNAKE MOUNTAIN

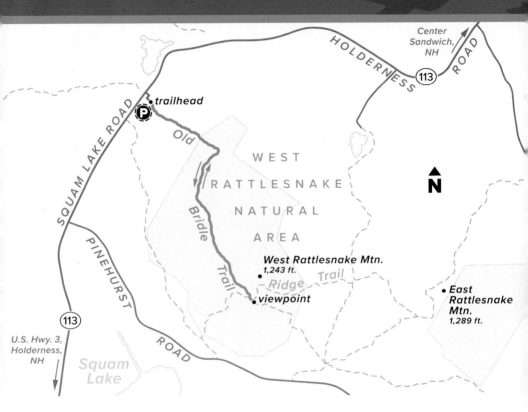

YOUR ADVENTURE

Adventurers, don't worry—there aren't any rattlesnakes on these ledges, though long ago timber rattlesnakes liked the warm rocks for basking. Today, you'll enjoy the warmth of the summit yourself and maybe find another kind of snake here on the historic homeland of the Abenaki. Start on the Old Bridle Trail, climbing up the stairs. Look out for stone walls as

LENGTH

1.9 miles

out and back

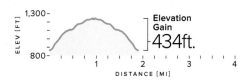

Elevation Gain

434ft.

HIKE + EXPLORE 1.5 hours

DIFFICULTY Moderate—gentle elevation gain, but a bit rooty; watch the exposed ledge

SEASON Year-round. May through October is best for clear days and fall colors; spring is quite muddy; road is plowed in winter but can close, so be sure to call.

GET THERE Take NH-113 / Squam Lake Road north from Holderness, and the parking lot will be on your right.

Google Maps: bit.ly/timberwestrattlesnake

RESTROOMS None

FEE None

TREAT YOURSELF Hot cocoa, egg sandwiches, grilled muffins, and coffee (for the adult adventurers) await at Mad River Coffee Roasters.

Squam Lakes Association
(603) 968-7336 | Instagram @Squam.Lakes
Facebook @SquamLakesAssociation

Take in the view at the top of West Rattlesnake Mountain

you walk, evidence of sheep pastures from the 1800s. Take a power-up on a big, flat boulder along the way. Once the trail flattens out, a large ledge suddenly emerges. Feel the rock and look for small pits where soft minerals have been weathered out. Power up here, enjoy the view of the islands in Squam Lake below, and head back the way you came.

SCAVENGER HUNT

Squam Lake islands

The Abenaki call this lake Keeseenunknipee, which means "goose lake in the highlands." Today it holds 6791 acres of water, thirty named islands, and more, smaller unnamed islands. From right to left, you might spot Sheep Island, Mink Island, Chocorua Island, Merrill Island, or the larger Long Island. Can you spot Five Finger Point to your left? What would you name your own island?

∧ How many islands can you count?

Garter snake

Watch for these reptiles in the leaves off the trail—recognize them by the three yellowish stripes running the length of their body. They aren't venomous, but, as with all wildlife, give them space. Snakes are cold-blooded, meaning they need help warming their bodies—garter snakes warm up by sitting in the sun. How do you warm up or cool down?

Thamnophis sirtalis ⌐

Common loon

Use binoculars to spot the loons' checkerboard backs in the lake below. Squam Lake's loon population has been declining, so the Loon Preservation Committee is trying to help them out by studying and raising awareness. Their initiative was the first to report about dangerous chemicals in unhatched loon eggs, and now there is an advisory on eating fish from the lake—a reminder that everything is connected.

Gavia immer >

Douglas's knotweed

These ledges are one of only about twelve spots in New Hampshire where you can find this yummy-smelling herb. Look for its long, hairless stems cropping up with small white flowers in summer. It likes thin, rocky soil.

< The rare *Polygonum douglasii*

Red oak

Look for the deep furrows of the red oak bark as you begin your hike. Do they look like ski trails to you? Grab an acorn from the ground and make it ski down the bark. Be sure to leave the acorn for a deer to eat later. The sharp, many-lobed leaves turn fiery red in fall. Fire skiing, anyone?

< *Quercus rubra*

38

SEEK THE SHELTER ON MOUNT MAJOR

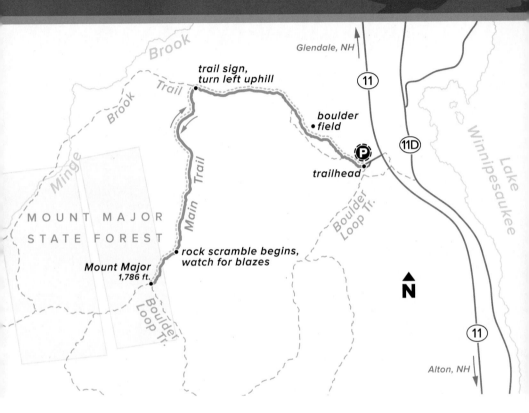

MOUNT MAJOR
STATE FOREST

Mount Major
1,786 ft.

trail sign,
turn left uphill

boulder
field

trailhead

rock scramble begins,
watch for blazes

Glendale, NH

11

11D

Lake Winnipesaukee

Brook

Brook Trail

Minge Brook

Main Trail

Boulder Loop Tr.

Boulder Loop Tr.

N

11

Alton, NH

YOUR ADVENTURE

Adventurers, today you'll climb on the easternmost peak of the Belknap Mountain Range in the historic homeland of the Abenaki. Start out with the blue blazes and pass a huge boulder on your right, then a few more until you reach a trail junction—these metamorphic rocks are 400 million years old. Take the blue-blazed Main Trail to the left. Power up, because it's going

LENGTH

2.8 miles

out and back

HIKE + EXPLORE 2 hours

DIFFICULTY Challenging—short, but has rolling ascents on smooth granite that might slow down smaller legs

SEASON Year-round.

GET THERE North of Alton on NH-11 / Mt Major Highway, turn west into the parking lot.

Google Maps: bit.ly/timbermountmajor

RESTROOMS At parking lot

FEE Suggested $5 donation via cash or QR code

TREAT YOURSELF Stillwells Ice Cream in Alton Bay has huge portions and tons of flavors, perfect for post-summit.

Society for the Protection of New Hampshire Forests

(603) 224-9945 | Facebook @ForestSociety

Soak in the view of Lake Winnipesaukee

to get steep, but worry not—it's short. Toward the end, there's a bit of a rock scramble, then the granite carpet rolls out in front of you. If it's raining or if it rained recently, be careful you don't slip on the wet rock. While you're up here, say thanks for stewardship—this is the idea of caring for lands so future visitors can enjoy them. Three organizations, the Society for the Protection of New Hampshire Forests, the Lakes Region Conservation Trust, and the Belknap Range Conservation Coalition, worked together to raise money for this land. Thanks, team!

SCAVENGER HUNT

Shelter remains

Welcome to the remains of Mr. Phippen's hut. George Phippen bought this land for $125 (!) and built this shelter for hikers in 1925. Unfortunately, wind blew the roof off twice, and the second time, in 1928, it was never replaced. Power up inside and pretend it's 1928—what would you sound like and what would you be talking about?

< What will you look like when you're 95?

Lake Winnipesaukee

In the Abenaki language, Winnipesaukee means "the smile of the great spirit" and refers to a great love story. Power up and look out toward the southern rim of the White Mountains. The lake was scooped out by that infamous receding glacier. How deep do you think it is?

The largest lake in New Hampshire >

Red eft

This is the juvenile stage of New Hampshire's state amphibian, the red-spotted newt. They like to come out after rain—look for a splash of bright red crossing your trail. The efts emerge from ponds in summer and live on land for two to seven years before retiring back to the pond as greenish adults. How will you change when you turn into an adult?

∧ *Notophthalmus viridescens*

Juniper bush

Find this aromatic bush growing around the summit and crush a few of its scaly needles, which grow in whorls of three, to release its scent. Open up a blue cone (looks like a berry) and count the seeds inside. How many seeds do you think one bush can grow?

Juniperus virginiana >

Geological survey marker

The National Geodetic Survey places brass disks like these at specific points to help them study Earth's shape and measure the distance between points (a science known as geodesy). Once you find one, count how many steps between it and the hut. You're now officially a land surveyor.

< Can you find two of these at the summit?

39

BLUEBERRY YOUR WAY TO BLUE JOB MOUNTAIN TOWER

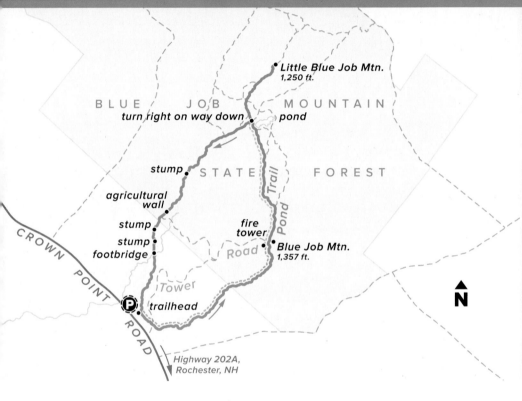

BLUE   JOB   MOUNTAIN

Little Blue Job Mtn.
1,250 ft.

turn right on way down   pond

STATE   FOREST

stump

agricultural
wall

stump   fire
                               tower
stump
footbridge   Blue Job Mtn.
                                      1,357 ft.

Road

Pond Trail

CROWN POINT ROAD

Tower

trailhead

Highway 202A,
Rochester, NH

N

YOUR ADVENTURE

Adventurers, you're in the Blue Hills on the historic homeland of the Penna-cook. The mountain you'll be hiking is named for Job (rhymes with globe) Allard, who owned land here. Start with the orange blazes and head up to the right, going counterclockwise on this loop. Take a left and conquer Blue Job's fire tower. At the top, see how many landforms you can identify—look for Mount Washington to the north, Mount Monadnock to the west, and

ELEV [FT]

1,400–

900–

Elevation Gain
365ft.

DISTANCE [MI]

1   2   3   4

Ready to climb
the tower?

LENGTH

2.2-mile reverse lollipop

HIKE + EXPLORE 1.5 hours

DIFFICULTY Moderate—short and sweet,
but the way up has some steepness and
tricky footing

SEASON Year-round. Best May through
October; late summer has blueberries
and fall has great hawk migration views.

GET THERE From NH-16, take 202A /
Walnut Street east to Crown Point Road
for 5.5 miles to find the parking area along
the right.

Google Maps: bit.ly/timberbluejob

RESTROOMS None

FEE None

TREAT YOURSELF Wild Willy's Burgers
has cowboy-themed fun waiting for you in
Rochester.

Blue Job Mountain State Forest,
New Hampshire Department of Natural
and Cultural Resources
(603) 271-2217 | Twitter @NHdncr

the Atlantic Ocean to the east. Power up, and head back down because your adventure isn't over yet. Pass the Tower Road on your left and keep going straight, following cairns and white blazes on bare rock—be careful not to go off track. Soon you'll reach a small, unnamed pond. What would you name it? Pass a turn to the left—you'll return to this soon—and follow small cairns until you reach the open granite summit of Little Blue Job Mountain, where you'll find a rock cairn and blueberry bushes. Pick some berries if they're in season, then turn around and head back. This time turn right at the pond you named to make your way down.

SCAVENGER HUNT

Blue Job Tower

Let's climb one of sixteen fire towers in New Hampshire—if you visit five, you can earn a patch from the Fire Tower Quest Program on nh.gov/nhdfl. In 1903, over 10 percent of the forests in the White Mountains burned in spring alone—it was called the "Year that New Hampshire Burned," and it started the fire tower movement. This steel tower with a wood cabin was built in 1915 and modified over the decades, but it is still in active use.

What would a forest fire look like from up here? ⌐

Seasonal special: broad-winged hawk

In September, you'll meet people with binoculars and tripods on Little Blue Job summit, watching for these birds of prey with a banded tail and wide wings. During the fall migration, you might see as many as 800 hawks. Bring your binoculars or politely ask to borrow a pair (birders are generally a friendly group).

∧ *Buteo platypterus*

Little Blue Job summit

After conquering the tower, be sure to make your way to the wide-open Little Blue Job summit. You walked through a saddle, a space between two mountains, to get here. Though many people like to add stones to cairns or build their own, rangers hope you won't— adding stones can unbalance the carefully built structures and disturb the summit ecosystem.

< The cairn that marks the summit

Seasonal special: lowbush blueberry

Two-thirds of this bush lives underground. That means even if a fire burns the top part, it can keep growing. Find these delicious berries July through September and snack on them to power up. After the berries disappear in fall, the leaves turn a gorgeous red and purple. It's the gift that keeps on giving. Foxes and bears like berries too, so stay aware as you forage.

Vaccinium angustifolium >

Moose scat

Keep an eye out for moose scat—you can tell moose scat is different than bear or other omnivore scat because moose are herbivores that fully digest their food. In bear or fox scat, you might see pieces of berries and other undigested food. Based on what they've left behind, who else has been on this trail?

< *Alces alces* poop

40

BRIDGE HOP TO PULPIT ROCK

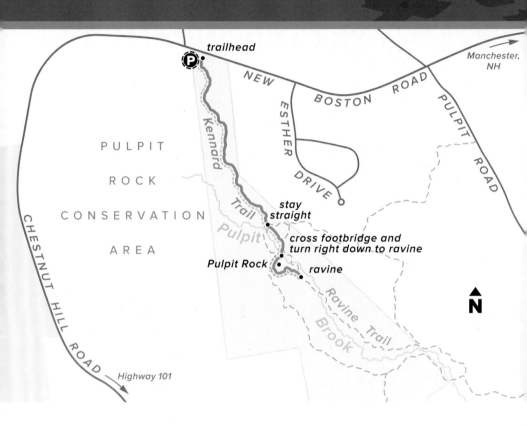

trailhead

Manchester, NH

NEW

ESTHER

BOSTON ROAD

PULPIT

DRIVE

ROAD

Kennard

Trail

PULPIT

ROCK

CONSERVATION

AREA

stay straight

cross footbridge and turn right down to ravine

Pulpit

Pulpit Rock

ravine

CHESTNUT HILL ROAD

Ravine Trail

Brook

N

Highway 101

YOUR ADVENTURE

Adventurers, welcome to the historic homeland of the Pennacook. Thousands of years ago, lakes held back by ice dams in the melting Laurentide Ice Sheet burst open, causing waterfalls that eroded the rock beneath and created the ravine you'll visit today. Start out on the white-blazed Kennard Trail. Wind gently through the forest, passing many footbridges (can you

LENGTH

1.8 miles

out and back

HIKE + EXPLORE 1.5 hours

DIFFICULTY Moderate—nice and short, with a little bit of a climb down to the bottom of ravine

SEASON Year-round. The parking lot is plowed in winter, but the trail can get icy, so be careful. Fall is best, as flies and mosquitoes can be bothersome in spring and summer.

GET THERE Take New Boston Road west from Bedford. The parking lot is on the south side of the road, after Esther Drive.

Google Maps: bit.ly/timberpulpit

RESTROOMS None

FEE None

TREAT YOURSELF Manchester's Cremeland Drive In has burgers and ice cream waiting for you.

Piscataquog Land Conservancy
(603) 487-3331
Instagram @PLC_NH
Facebook @PLCNH

One of many footbridges you'll take to the ravine

count them all?) and follow the signs to the ravine. You'll pass two red trails going left—stay straight—then you'll reach the top and the pulpit. Be careful here and stay back from the precipice. Take the orange trail to the right and cross another footbridge, then go down to the bottom of the ravine, watching your step. Power up here and head back the way you came.

SCAVENGER HUNT

Pulpit Rock ledge

This "pulpit" created by glacial flooding looks like a platform where you might give a lecture or sermon. Write a story in your nature journal about a woodland creature giving a presentation to fellow creatures below in the ravine. What kind of animal is it? What is it saying?

Observe from afar and imagine yourself in the audience >

Ravine

As giant ice dams on glacial lakes melted around 14,000 years ago, they released huge amounts of water and sediment very quickly. Sand, pebbles, and even boulder-sized rocks got caught in what probably started as a small pothole and swirled around, creating the ravine. Check out the sand and rocks down here—how many different kinds can you find?

< The quietness at the bottom of the ravine

Snowshoe hare

You might get lucky and spot this color-changing mammal with wide tracks that look like a snowshoe. They'll be brown in summer and white in winter to camouflage in the snow. Use some sticks to make wide snowshoe tracks like the hare's.

< *Lepus americanus*

Kennard Trail

According to Richard Moore, chairman of Bedford Conservation Commission's Pulpit Rock Subcommittee, "Dr. John Kennard dreamed for a long time of preserving Pulpit Rock as a conservation area. Unfortunately, he passed away before he could make it happen, but other members of the commission worked hard to bring Dr. Kennard's dream to fruition." Say thanks to all of them for helping create this trail.

∧ Find the trail sign

Partridge berry

Look for the shiny, rounded leaves of this vine and its white flowers that grow in pairs in spring and fuse into a berry in summer and fall. Lots of animals like the berry—do you see any sign of animals around?

< *Mitchella repens* (in Latin, *repens* means "creeping")

41

WALK THE ROCKS AT ODIORNE POINT STATE PARK

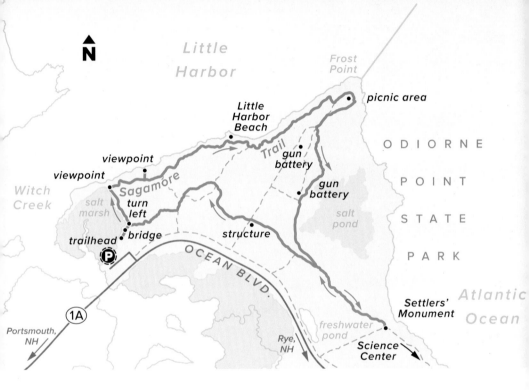

YOUR ADVENTURE

Adventurers, you're at a spot the Abenaki call "place where the waters of the ocean spread out." Settler John Odiorne arrived here in 1660, and generations of his family lived and farmed here until World War II. From the parking lot, cross the bridge with the salt marsh on your left and turn left to begin your loop. Head straight for your first shore viewpoint, then

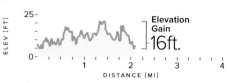

Can you walk the point?

LENGTH

2.1-mile loop

HIKE + EXPLORE 1.5

DIFFICULTY Easy—nice and flat and not too long; be sure stay on the trail

SEASON Year-round. Swimming in summer; snowshoeing in winter. Staffing depends on weather.

GET THERE Take NH-1A toward the ocean until you find the Odiorne Point Boat Launch parking lot on your left (lot closed in winter; park at Science Center).

Google Maps: bit.ly/timberodiorne

RESTROOMS None

FEE $4 adults, $6 kids 6–11, free for kids under 6

TREAT YOURSELF Get a hot popover with maple butter at Popovers on the Square in Portsmouth.

Odiorne Point State Park
(603) 436-7406
Instagram @NHStateParks
Facebook @NewHampshireStateParks

come back on the trail and turn left. Keep hiking for a bit and take another power-up at a shore viewpoint. At just about half a mile, come out onto Little Harbor Beach and follow that all the way to Frost Point. Carefully rock hop your way to the tip. Power up at the benches and picnic tables on the grass facing the point, then continue behind the grass and take the trail to explore one of two WWII gun batteries—head back to the main trail to see the second one. Keep straight, passing the route back home for the moment to go all the way down to the Settlers' Monument, then turn around and stay straight to begin your return, passing a WWII bunker and ending up at the bridge and marsh again.

SCAVENGER HUNT

Battery Seaman

Military planners in World War II, worried the Germans would attack Portsmouth, took over Odiorne Point and built gun bunkers as part of Fort Dearborn. Most of the New Hampshire coastline is sand or marsh, and this was one of the few points high enough to build a defense on. Luckily, the war never came to this shore, and the guns only fired once as a test. It became a state park in 1961.

∧ One of two concrete Panama mounts that held guns

Settlers' Monument

Can you imagine the first English settlers arriving in New Hampshire on this spot in 1623? Take a moment and write in your journal what someone might have thought as they first arrived here. What would you notice?

An 8000-pound monument >

Shagbark hickory

If there are many of these big, rounded leaves on the trail, choose one to take home. Put it in water for a week, then take it out and carefully push out the green parts to reveal the veins and make a "leaf skeleton" to glue in your nature journal. In September and October, look for nuts—they start out bright green

before turning brown. Animals snack on them, so you may find the husk with the nut missing. Be sure to stay on the trail through this delicate area.

Carya ovata (in Latin, "nut-bearing" and "rounded") ⁊

Staghorn sumac

In winter and early spring, you can see how these squiggly, hairy branches resemble antlers. Through summer, the long, lance-shaped leaves grow opposite each other in rows. Their flowers bloom in June and July, then give way to fuzzy red berries birds love in fall. Stand with your head in front of the branches so they look like your antlers.

< *Rhus typhina*

Painted lady butterfly

Look for the four "eyespots" on the underside of this orange, black, and white butterfly. You'll find it in spring and fall out in sunny, open fields as it stops over on its migration from the Southwest states—it especially loves plants like thistle. See if you can re-create its beautiful wing pattern in your nature journal.

< *Vanessa cardui*

ADVENTURES IN
MAINE

Dirigo, adventurers. This state motto means "I guide" in Latin, and refers to the North Star depicted on Maine's flag. Guide your crew through the Pine Tree State, which is over 90 percent forested, the most forest of any state, and dream about the day you summit Mount Katahdin, terminus of the 2064-mile Appalachian Trail and highest point in the state at 5267 feet. Maine entered the Union as the twenty-third state in 1820. That is its recent, human history. Remember to look for its geologic history—500 million years ago, molten rock pushed toward the surface to create the mountains all around you. The Laurentide Ice Sheet that shaped southern New England also left its mark here. As you hike along the coastal lowlands, imagine sea level being much lower and yourself standing on mountains. Your adventure starts in the White Mountains near New Hampshire before passing through the New England uplands in the middle of the state and ending Downeast in the coastal lowlands, where you can walk to the most easterly spot in the whole United States.

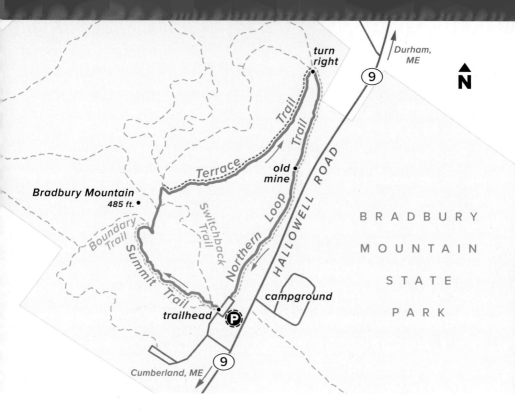

YOUR ADVENTURE

Adventurers, you're on the historic homeland of the Wabanaki, who camped here on trips to the coast. It's time to bag a nice, easy peak in a state park that's been around since 1940. You'll be traveling clockwise, starting by the playground, and heading up, up, up on the Summit Trail for a short while until stone staircases suddenly reveal your destination—the granite

LENGTH

1.2-mile

loop

700–

ELEV [FT]

200–

Elevation Gain

248ft.

1   2   3   4

DISTANCE [MI]

HIKE + EXPLORE 1 hour

DIFFICULTY Moderate—steep uphill, but short and doable; gentle downhill

SEASON Year-round. The annual Hawk Watch takes place mid-March through mid-May. Winter is beautifully quiet (be sure to bring snowshoes or spikes).

GET THERE Heading north on ME-9, the state park entrance will be on your left.

Google Maps: bit.ly/timberbradbury

RESTROOMS At parking lot

FEE $1 kids 5–11, $4 adult ME residents, free for residents 65 and over, $6 adult nonresidents

TREAT YOURSELF Wicked Whoopies in Freeport has a dozen flavors of mini pies, the perfect size for a post-hike snack.

Bradbury Mountain State Park,
Maine Department of Agriculture,
Conservation, and Forestry
(207) 688-4712
Facebook @MaineDACF

Nothing beats a bare-rock summit

summit! Be careful near the edges and enjoy basking like a lizard on the warm rock as you power up and take in the 360-degree views. Park manager Chris Silsbee likes visiting in the fall because, "from the summit, you can view the diversity of fall colors up and down the coast of Maine." Keep going across the summit—imagine a glacier rolling by and scraping the rock into the shape you see today. Pass the yellow-blazed Boundary Trail and then the Switchback Trail—take your next right turn on the Terrace Trail, which meanders down on a gentle slope to your final right on the Northern Loop. Look out for old agricultural walls signaling that this used to be farmland and, in the 1920s, a mine for feldspar used to make porcelain dishes. Consider camping at the nearby park campground.

SCAVENGER HUNT

Feldspar crystals

Bradbury Mountain is made up of white granite and pegmatite—look closely at the rocks under your feet at the summit. Pick up the sparkly pieces and imagine using them to make pottery in the 1920s—there used to be a quarry here along the trail.

Feel the grains of granite >

Wild sarsaparilla

Look for the compound leaflets of three to five finely toothed leaves year-round. A cluster of white flowers appears in spring, which turns into blue-black berries in summer. Take a whiff—it smells pretty good. The roots are sometimes used to make a kind of root beer.

< *Aralia nudicaulis*

Bloody brittlegill

Check for this showy gilled mushroom underneath the conifer (cone-bearing) trees along the trail. Feel its gills gently—can you understand how they got their name? When you get home, use some Play-Doh to recreate the design of the gills. What do they remind you of?

< Russula sanguinaria

Pine tree spur-throat grasshopper

Watch for these insects on rocks and under pine trees. They love to eat leaves and sometimes even pine needles—drop a few on a rock and see what happens. Grasshoppers can jump over 3 feet. If you could jump as far as a grasshopper relative to your size, you could spring over nine school busses in one bound!

Melanoplus punctulatus >

Goldenrod

Look for these tall yellow flowers with long lance-like leaves during summer and fall. Goldenrod grows in large stands or colonies with its buddies. Its long spears of flowers are called inflorescences. Watch one for at least two minutes. Are any bees coming by to pollinate? Why might a bee like these?

< Solidago species

FIND THE SECRET OASIS AT RATTLESNAKE POOL

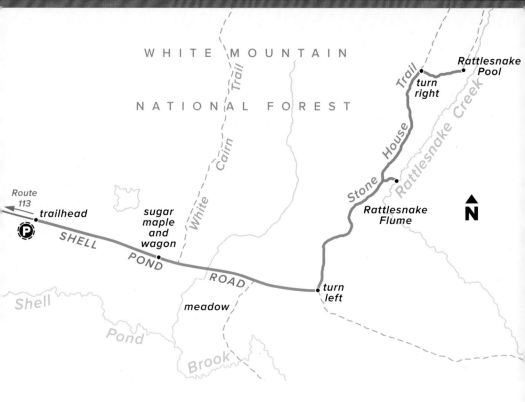

YOUR ADVENTURE

Adventurers, you're searching for a beautiful, cold, green pool on the historic homeland of the Wabanaki, in an area known today as Evans Notch. *Notch* means a low point in a ridge, and this one cuts through the White Mountains, the rugged, 87-mile portion of the Appalachian Range that extends through New Hampshire and southwestern Maine. Start

The pool is always beautiful and never warm

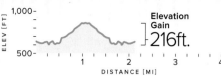

1,000–

ELEV [FT]

500–

Elevation Gain
216ft.

1   2   3   4

DISTANCE [MI]

LENGTH

2.1 miles out and back

HIKE + EXPLORE 1.5 hours

DIFFICULTY Moderate—short, with just a small push up to the pool

SEASON Year-round. Shell Pond Road is plowed in winter. May through October is best for a nice quick swim—the water is cold!

GET THERE From Route 113, head east on Stone House Road / Shell Pond Road for 1 mile (after going over the bridge, bear right, ignoring the dirt road going left). Park at the gate.

Google Maps: bit.ly/timberrattlesnakepool

RESTROOMS At parking lot

FEE None

TREAT YOURSELF Stow Corner Store, south on Route 113 / Stow Road, has yummy ice cream and pizza for the end of your adventure.

White Mountain National Forest
(603) 536-6100
Instagram @WhiteMountainForest
Facebook @WhiteMountainNF

your adventure after the parking gate, walking on a dirt road alongside a meadow. Remember that everything past the gate is private property. The landowners have generously allowed this area to stay open to the public, so let's respect their wishes by staying on marked trails and following signs. Turn left on the Stone House Trail—you'll see a sign for Rattlesnake Pool in about half a mile. Take your first right to view the flume from a wooden bridge over Rattlesnake Creek. Head back to the main trail and continue up until you find the sign pointing right to Rattlesnake Pool. Take in the view of the pool from above. Be careful on the rooty descent down to the cool water. Power up here as long as you'd like and head back the way you came.

SCAVENGER HUNT

Giant sugar maple

If you're here in fall, check out the beautiful array of colors that this giant sugar maple goes through—green to bright red to orange to yellow. Note the leaves' three pointy lobes and touch the bark. Any sticky spots? Delicious maple syrup comes from these trees. The old wagon under this tree has been on the property for a long time—any guesses how long?

Acer saccharum >

Rattlesnake Flume

The walls of the flume are hard volcanic, or igneous, rock that resisted erosion as water wore away the rock between them. Glacial flooding probably helped, washing sediment, called till, all the way down to the Shell Pond area. The bridge over the flume is perfect for power-ups.

Check out the 10-foot plunge >

Rattlesnake Pool

Peer into the emerald depths of this glacial pothole. See the boulders at the bottom? Glacial floods swirled small rocks around in a hole in the bedrock until it got bigger, eventually capturing larger rocks and boulders, and swirling and swirling until they had carved out this deep, round pool.

< Ready for a cool dip?

Bigtooth aspen

Deciduous trees like this lose their leaves in winter. Watch them tremble in the wind up high or, in autumn, find their toothy yellow spade shapes on the ground. Take one home and try a negative-space painting—put it on paper and paint all around, then take it away to reveal a silhouette with a toothy border.

< *Populus grandidentata*

American beech

This is another deciduous tree with toothed leaves. What is different about these leaves and the aspen leaves? Find a nice narrow one on the ground to use as a boat and help your hiking buddy find one too. Choose a finish line downstream and release your boats at the same time to see whose is the fastest.

< *Fagus grandifolia*

"THRU-HIKE" TO TABLE ROCK

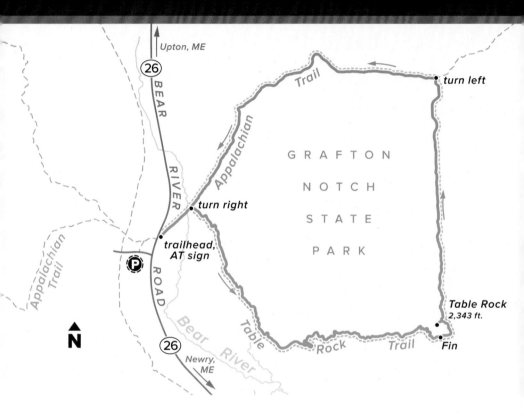

YOUR ADVENTURE

Adventurers, today you're hiking on the Appalachian Trail. Carefully cross the street, take a selfie with the AT sign, and you're off! You'll cross some footbridges then hit a fork—turn right to climb up the rocky, steep-but-fun orange-blazed trail. You'll negotiate the boulders left behind from the Laurentide Ice Sheet and go up, down, and around—there are even chutes and ladders with iron rungs to climb, so take your time and be careful.

∧ Count the iron rungs
you tackle today

LENGTH

2.4-mile loop

HIKE + EXPLORE 2.5 hours

DIFFICULTY Challenging—tricky rock crevice, but it is so cool; worth it if you take your time; might be too difficult for under-sevens

SEASON Year-round, but winter is difficult and icy; May through October for gorgeous views.

GET THERE The Appalachian Trail parking lot is on the west side of ME-26 in Grafton Notch State Park.

Google Maps: bit.ly/timbertablerock

RESTROOMS At parking lot

FEE $1 kids 5–11, $3 adult ME residents, free for residents 65 and over, $4 adult nonresidents, $1 senior nonresidents

TREAT YOURSELF It's the honor system at Puzzle Mountain Bakery stand, a few minutes south on the west side of the road. Drop some cash and take a pie, whoopie pie, or maple cookies.

Grafton Notch State Park, Maine Department of Agriculture, Conservation, and Forestry in season: (207) 824-2912, off season: (207) 624-6080 | Facebook @MaineDACF

After a few ladders, find yourself at the lookout. Power up at Table Rock. When you're done, continue on the blue-blazed trail, down a few more iron rungs to meet back up with the Appalachian Trail. Turn left, and it will gradually take you past your first fork to the orange trail you came up. Cross the highway again and high five your hiking buddy—you hiked on the AT!

SCAVENGER HUNT

Table Rock

You made it! This granite you're standing on is over 400 million years old. State geologist Robert Marvinney says, "Maine's rocks and landscapes record more than a billion years of Earth's history. Written in the rocks is the story of building up of massive mountain ranges, now worn down for millions of years by rain, wind, and primarily glacial ice, which scoured the landscape to create thousands of pristine lakes, and Maine's exquisite rocky coastline."

Climb over 400 million years of geologic history >

The Fin

Weather and the freeze-thaw cycle shaped all the small caves and boulders you so bravely climbed up to get here. When water gets into a crack in a rock and freezes, it expands. If this happens over and over, it can create a bigger crack or even break the rock apart. When you get home, fill a plastic cup to the top with water and put it in the freezer. What does it look like when you check on it a day later?

Look for this just before your final climb to the top of Table Rock >

Old Speck

Be careful at the rocky lookout while you enjoy the view of Maine's fourth-highest mountain. Do you see the four vertical scrapes with no trees on the near slope? Those are from old landslides— scars from living that long mountain life. Look down at your knees. Do you have any scars?

A view of Old Speck, 4170 feet >

Appalachian Trail thru-hikers

Look for hikers passing with big (really big) packs. Millions hike parts of the AT every year, but only a few hundred complete the whole thing. From here to the end at Mount Katahdin in Maine is about 267 miles— could you do it? How about hiking south to the end in Georgia—nearly 2000 miles away! Be a "trail angel" and pack an extra snack for a hungry thru-hiker. Ask them their trail name and make up one for yourself. It can be an inside joke or just something you like. Peanut Butter? Dinosaur?

This sign marks the final leg of the Appalachian Trail >

Gymnopilus mushroom

Find these gilled mushrooms poking out of trees with their buddies. Every once in a while, you'll spot one growing all alone. Why do you think this is? Would you rather grow up by yourself or in a group?

< *Gymnopilus luteus*

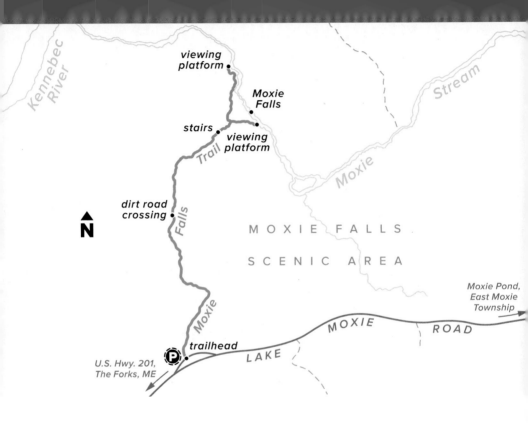

YOUR ADVENTURE

Adventurers, welcome to the historic homeland of the Wabanaki. You're about to descend on some sweet boardwalks to Moxie ("dark water" in Abenaki) Falls. Moxie Stream flows out of Moxie Pond and feeds into the 170-mile-long Kennebec River. On your way down, you'll cross a dirt road. Wind down boardwalks, stop at a viewing platform, soak in the 30-foot

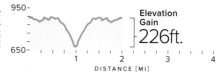

ELEV [FT]

950–

650–

Elevation Gain

226ft.

1   2   3   4

DISTANCE [MI]

Follow the boardwalks to the viewing deck for the 80-foot plunge

LENGTH

2 miles out and back

HIKE + EXPLORE 1 hour

DIFFICULTY Easy—straight shot with gradual down and up on boardwalks and wide trails

SEASON Year-round. May to June has the strongest water flow and wildflowers.

GET THERE Head east on Lake Moxie Road from Highway 201 for 3 miles to find the parking lot and trailhead on your left.

Google Maps: bit.ly/timbermoxie

RESTROOMS At parking lot

FEE None

TREAT YOURSELF South on Highway 201, Kennebec River Brewery has yummy burgers and fries, plus blueberry beer for adult adventurers.

Maine Department of Agriculture, Conservation, and Forestry

(207) 624-6077

Facebook @MaineDACF

upper falls and gorge, then keep going to a second viewing deck where you can check out the 80-foot drop of the main falls. Try to sketch the falls in your nature journal. Return the way you came.

SCAVENGER HUNT

Moxie Stream and Falls

This black metamorphic slate that Moxie Stream flows over is from the Silurian period, 443 to 416 million years ago. What's the oldest thing you own? Moxie Stream flows into the powerful 170-mile-long Kennebec River, the longest river that runs entirely in Maine.

The upper falls surrounded by early autumn colors >

Balsam poplar

These wide, toothy leaves turn yellow in fall. Gather the brightest ones on the ground and spell your name on the boardwalk. If you're here in spring, take a deep breath. Smell that Christmassy balsam scent? The tree's buds are covered with a protective sap—when they open in spring, the scent wafts far and wide.

< *Populus balsamifera*

Northern white cedar

Look for the stringy bark and telltale scaly leaves of this tree. Fragrant cedar wood has long been used for building—lots of log cabins are made from cedar. Find some nice-smelling sticks on the ground and play "rhythm sticks." Someone taps two sticks together in a pattern and the rest of the group matches, then someone else starts a new rhythm.

Thuja occidentalis ⌐

Canadian bunchberry

This little plant has ridged leaves that grow in fours. You can spot it growing in carpets year-round. In late spring and summer, it has white flowers, which turn into bright red berries as fall approaches. Can you imagine if the carpet in your house grew flowers and berries?

< Cornus canadensis

Turkey tail mushroom

These polypores are a bracket fungi. They create a shelf on decaying wood and help break it down into new soil. Look for them from June through November. Some people make fancy jewelry out of these. How would you want to wear your fungus finery?

< Trametes ochracea

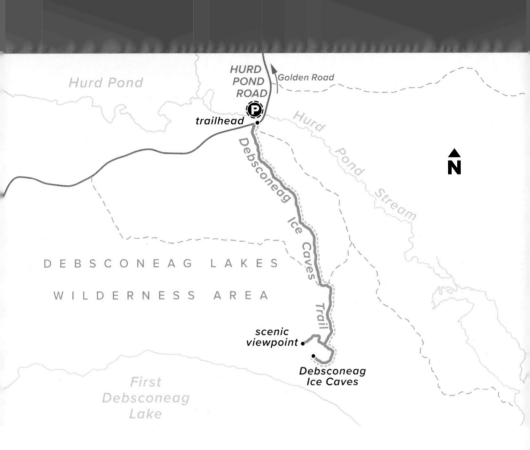

YOUR ADVENTURE

Adventurers, get ready to go spelunking on the historic homeland of the Penobscot. In their language, Debsconeag means "carrying place." Canoe travelers passing through must portage their boats from one lake to the next. Feel lucky you don't have to haul a canoe today! We'll start out following blue blazes as the trail gently goes up and down. Soon, you'll find a fairy

∧ Are you ready to take the cave challenge?

LENGTH 2.4 miles out and back

HIKE + EXPLORE 2 hours

DIFFICULTY Moderate—rocks and roots

SEASON Year-round, however road is gated and not plowed in winter. Spring is muddy and black flies are in full force May to early June. The cave has a lot of ice until late summer so best to wait until then if you want to go all the way in safely.

GET THERE From Millinocket, take Golden Road to Hurd Pond Road, just after Abol Bridge and Campground. Turn left and follow 4 miles to the Ice Caves Trail parking area on your right. After parking, cross the bridge to find the trailhead on the east side of the road.

Google Maps: bit.ly/timbericecaves

RESTROOMS There's an outhouse about 100 yards before the parking lot

FEE None

TREAT YOURSELF Whoopie pies and sandwiches at Katahdin General Store in Millinocket on Bates Street.

Debsconeag Lakes Wilderness Area, The Nature Conservancy
(207) 729-5181 | Facebook @TNCMaine

wonderland, a series of ginormous granite boulders topped with ferns—glacial erratics dropped from the Laurentide Ice Sheet thousands of years ago. You'll climb over them, past them, and between them. At a junction, you can choose a scenic overlook or the Ice Caves—let's go to the caves first. Turn left and wind down until you see the cave among the boulders—you'll recognize it from the bars marking the entrance and the iron rung ladder disappearing down. If you'd like, have an adult head down first using the rope as a guide. Down here, there is sometimes ice as late as August! If it looks like too much, just enjoy from afar. When you're done, head back up to the junction—now you're ready to power up at the scenic viewpoint overlooking First Debsconeag Lake. Return to your car the way you came.

SCAVENGER HUNT

The Ice Cave

This is a talus cave, caused by rocks spalling (chipping) off the cliffs above you and piling on the slope below. How many rocks do you think are in this talus pile? Exploring caves is called spelunking. On a hot day, spelunk this cave to enjoy nature's air-conditioning. Why do you think it is so much cooler inside the cave than out?

< Ready to spelunk?

Orange jelly spot mushroom

Some mushrooms are gilled, some are polypores, and some are weird jellies

like this one. Jelly spot likes to grow on decaying or dying wood, so if you see it on a tree, the tree may not be totally healthy. What other clues tell you a tree could be sick? Make up a new word to describe the mushroom's unique orange color.

< *Dacrymyces chrysospermus*

First Debsconeag Lake

When you turn right at the first junction, you're treated to this view of First Debsconeag Lake, the second largest of the chain lakes. The lakes are fed by the 117-mile-long West Branch Penobscot River, and they're home to lake trout and Atlantic salmon. Farther to the east you can see Debsconeag Deadwater.

< Power up at this great viewpoint

Stag's horn club moss

There are many different kinds of mosses and ferns on this adventure—look closely at one of the boulders for these tall green noodles. Mosses are ancient and simple plants. They are nonvascular, which means they don't have roots, veins, or other tubes to carry nutrients, so they can't get very big and need a lot of moisture to grow. Walk your fingers through the club moss forest and imagine what it would look like if you were tiny.

< *Lycopodium clavatum*

Seasonal special: American beech pod

Look for the spiny husks of this protein- and fat-rich nut, which almost every animal in this forest likes to snack on in fall. Gather as many as you can and have a bowling contest. Who can roll theirs the farthest? If all the nuts have been eaten, you might only find empty husk "wrappers"—tell the animals to clean up after themselves!

< *Fagus grandifolia* husk

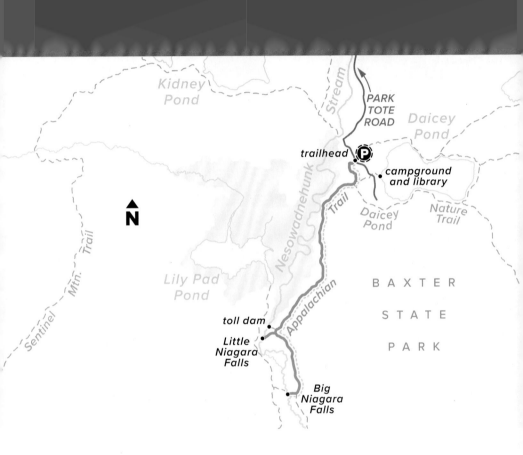

YOUR ADVENTURE

Adventurers, what's the biggest gift you've ever given someone? In 1937, former governor Percival Baxter gifted this entire 200,000-acre park to the public. He worked hard over many years to slowly purchase land for the park. Give him a quick thanks as you get out of your car at Daicey Pond. Here in Wabanaki Territory, you'll start your adventure on the Appalachian

Nesowadnehunk Stream tumbles through Little Niagara Falls

LENGTH

2.4 miles out and back

HIKE + EXPLORE 1.5 hours

DIFFICULTY Moderate—short with gradual inclines, roots, rocks, and plank crossings; keep littles close at waterfalls

SEASON Year-round, but you'll need skis in winter. May to October is best for waterfall flow.

GET THERE From Millinocket, take Millinocket Road to Baxter Park Road. Pass through the Togue Pond Gatehouse and stay to your left to take Park Tote Road for 10 miles until you reach Daicey Pond Road. Turn left. Trailhead parking is a mile down on your right.

Google Maps: bit.ly/timberniagara

RESTROOMS At parking lot

FEE Free for ME residents, $15 for nonresidents

TREAT YOURSELF The Appalachian Trail Cafe in Millinocket has a sundae with 14 scoops of ice cream (one for each AT state) on a donut, meant for those who finish all 2181 miles. They also have breakfast sandwiches and donuts *sans* ice cream.

Baxter State Park Authority

(207) 723-5140 | Facebook @BaxterStatePark

Trail, just like hundreds of hard-core hikers do every year. Follow the white blazes the whole way—they're super easy to find and the trail is clear. Sign the register and begin, crossing planks until you reach a fork with the Daicey Pond Nature Trail. Go right and follow the trail as it goes up, down, flattens out, then turn right on a side trail to arrive at the 17-mile Nesowadnehunk Stream and the remains of a dam. Check it out and power up, then head back and turn right to reach the Little Niagara Falls side trail—walk down, power up, and head back to the main trail. A short way along, you'll see the sign to Big Niagara Falls—turn right, head down, and take in the power! Consider camping at Daicey Pond as a reward; there are cute cabins and a library.

SCAVENGER HUNT

American red squirrel

Take a moment to sit on one of the rocks as you hike and watch for these tree-dwelling rodents. They are omnivorous, which means they eat both plants and meat. Around here, they like to snack on the sap from twigs. Will you be having an omnivorous snack at lunch?

Tamiasciurus hudsonicus (in Greek, "the steward who sits in the shadow of his tail") >

Scarlet waxcap

You can't miss this waxy-capped, yellow-gilled mushroom. It shines like a gummy bear on the forest floor in summer and fall. Do you have a color this red among your crayons or markers at home?

Hygrocybe coccinea (in Latin, "watery head" and "scarlet red") >

Moose

The word *moose* comes from an Algonquian term meaning "twig-eater." From mid-May through July and again in the fall mating season, you might be lucky and spot one of Maine's 75,000 moose. Watch quietly by the water at dusk or dawn when they are most active and keep a respectful distance. While hiking, keep

an eye out for their round balls of scat, larger than a deer's. Be careful driving, as they sometimes walk along the logging trails and cross roads.

Alces alces is Maine's state animal ⌐

Big Niagara Falls

Watch these falls cut through the 400-million year-old Katahdin granite and take in the view from the broad rock outcrops. Can you find West Peak and Doubletop Mountain in the distance? Feel the mist on your face and appreciate the power of all the snowmelt and other water rushing off Mount Katahdin.

The falls at the end of your hike >

Second Falls Below Toll Dam on Nesowadnehunk

Old toll dam

Look out at what remains of the old toll dam. It was built in 1879 for the timber industry. River drivers used poles to push logs downstream to the Penobscot West Branch River. It cost 63 cents for 1000 feet of logs. Send a twig downstream and pretend it's a log on its journey.

⌐ Imagine tall tree trunks floating through here

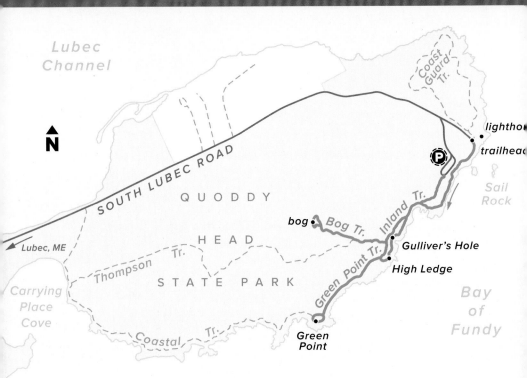

YOUR ADVENTURE

Adventurers, welcome to Quoddy Head, a name that means "beautiful and fertile place" to the Passamaquoddy people. It's also known as the Bold Coast—can you guess why? Your adventure starts on the coastal trail to the south of the red-and-white lighthouse. Roll along the flat Inland Trail, the easternmost portion of the United States. Stop and power up at benches

LENGTH

2.8 miles

Y-shaped out and back

ELEV [FT] · 125 · 0 · DISTANCE [MI] · 1 · 2 · 3 · 4

Elevation Gain **114ft.**

HIKE + EXPLORE 1.5 hours

DIFFICULTY Easy—some hand-holding spots near the ledges of the Inland Trail

SEASON May 15 through October 15.

GET THERE Take South Lubec Road for 4.6 miles south of Lubec as it curves to the end of Quoddy Head. Trailhead parking is to the right down a short dirt road.

Google Maps: bit.ly/timberquoddy

RESTROOMS At parking lot

FEE $1 kids 5–11, $3 adult ME residents, free for residents 65 or older, $4 adult nonresidents, $1 senior nonresidents

TREAT YOURSELF Monica's Chocolates in Lubec has clam-shaped confections.

Quoddy Head State Park,
Maine Department of Agriculture,
Conservation, and Forestry
(207) 733-0911 in season
(207) 941-4014 off season
Facebook @MaineDACF

West Quoddy
Head Lighthouse

along the way, watching the water for seagulls, whales, and porpoises. Check out Gulliver's Hole, then keep going to High Ledge, where you can lunch on spongy meadow grass (careful near the edges). Continue on Green Point Trail to take in the view and look for whales in summer. On the way back, follow signs to the Bog Trail. Turn left, and you'll come upon the bog, a special place with plants that can handle cold, acidic, and low-oxygen conditions. Do the lollipop bog loop, then turn left to take the Inland Trail back to the lighthouse. If you're up for more adventure, take the Coast Guard Trail from the parking lot for a nice half-mile loop down to the shore and back.

SCAVENGER HUNT

Fog

The park is often wreathed in fog. It forms when warm moist air from land meets the cold air over the ocean. Fog and sea breezes can make for a chilly, wet day—even in summer—so bring extra layers and walk carefully so you don't slip.

How's the visibility today? >

Purple pitcher plant

This carnivorous bog plant creates a fluid in its jug that smells sweet to attract insects. Once a bug crawls in, it slides down the smooth sides of the plant and lands in the fluid where special enzymes digest it and feed the plant. Play pitcher plant at lunch—fill your mouth with water and pretend a peanut or cracker is a fly—nom nom nom.

Sarracenia purpurea >

The gabbro of High Ledge and Gulliver's Hole

Take a peek down at Gulliver's Hole, an 80-foot chasm where water has eroded the black cliffs. These rocks formed from magma 420 million years ago, cooling slowly underground. Over time, the rocks above eroded away, revealing the smooth black rocks you see today. Power up on grassy High Ledge and look out over the Bay of Fundy, one of the seven wonders of North America and the place with the highest tides in the world.

< Look for these two geologic wonders at the hike's end

Orange lichen

Look for this orange lichen growing on rocks all around you. Though it looks leafy, it's not a plant; it's a symbiotic relationship between fungi and algae— the algae make food and the fungi protect the algae. The orange color of this lichen is actually a kind of sunscreen that allows them to live on sunny rocks.

Xanthoria parietina >

Mountain ash

Look for this tree's compound (multiple leaves on a stalk), toothy leaves year-round. It has white flowers from late spring to early summer and bright red berries from late summer through winter. Sit and watch quietly— do any bees visit the flowers? Any birds or squirrels come by to munch the berries?

< *Sorbus americana* berries

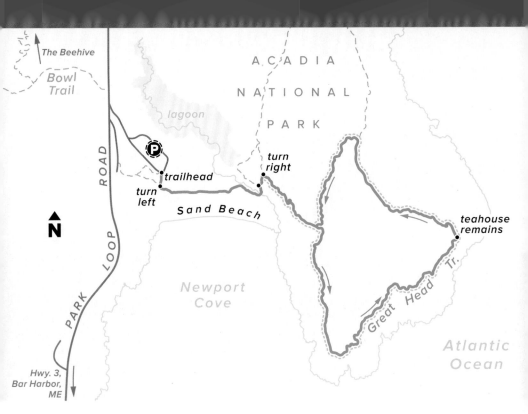

The Beehive

Bowl Trail

lagoon

A C A D I A

N A T I O N A L

P A R K

turn
right

ROAD

trailhead

turn
left

Sand Beach

teahouse
remains

N

PARK   LOOP

Newport
Cove

Great Head Tr.

Atlantic
Ocean

Hwy. 3,
Bar Harbor,
ME

YOUR ADVENTURE

Adventurers, get ready to circle the Great Head on the historic homelands
of the Wabanaki. Start in the Sand Beach parking lot and take the stairs
down to the beach. Turn left and cross the sand to feel the water in the
lagoon. What does it feel like? Find the opening in the forest with a sign for
the Great Head Trail and climb a series of granite steps—how many can you

LENGTH

1.4-mile

lollipop loop

Elevation Gain
132ft.

ELEV [FT] — 250 — 0

DISTANCE [MI] — 1 — 2 — 3 — 4

HIKE + EXPLORE 1.5 hours

DIFFICULTY Moderate—short, but rolling ascents on smooth granite might slow down little legs

SEASON Spring through fall. Park Loop Road closes from December to mid-April.

GET THERE Take Park Loop Road south from Bar Harbor to the Sand Beach entrance gate and find the parking lot on your left. (Note: Park Loop Road is one-way.)

Google Maps: bit.ly/timbergreathead

RESTROOMS At parking lot

FEE $30 per vehicle; purchase at the entry on Park Loop Road or online at recreation.gov

TREAT YOURSELF Get an original popover and ice cream at Jordan Pond House, off Park Loop Road.

Acadia National Park

(207) 288-3338 | Facebook @AcadiaNPS

The view of Sand Beach from Great Head

count? Be sure to follow the blue blazes painted on the rock until you reach a fork with a wooden sign. Take the loop counterclockwise until you reach the highest point and the old foundation of Satterlee Teahouse. Use the map to find as many landmarks as you can in Newport Cove, including Old Soaker, a chunk of rocks where seals love to hang out. Keep going until you reach the top of the stairs back to the beach and consider camping out at Blackwoods Campground just a few miles south.

SCAVENGER HUNT

Pink granite

Look closely at this area's 400-million-year-old granite. Each different grain you see is a crystal that formed slowly from hot magma. The slower the magma cooled, the bigger the crystal. How many colors can you see? Acadia's granite cliffs are pink because they contain lots of crystals from the mineral feldspar.

Pretty pink granite >

Beehive Mountain

The Beehive is a roche moutonnée (French for "fleecy rock"), a rock formation that's lop-sided from a glacier scraping over the top. See how one side is smooth and sloping and the other side steep and rough? As the glacier slid up the sloping side, it smoothed the rock, but eventually it got stuck. In order to move again, it had to rip big pieces of rock away, creating the steep side. Point in the direction the glacier must've been moving.

∧ Would you want to climb that 539-foot rock?

Tea on the summit

In 1910, the famous banker J. P. Morgan bought this land for his daughter, and they built a teahouse right at the summit of Great Head. It burned down in the great fire of 1947, and only the foundation remains. His granddaughter, Eleanor Satterlee, donated the land to the national park. Sip some imaginary tea in her honor. Draw your own teahouse in your nature journal.

< Can you find the remains of the teahouse?

Beach rose

These prickly shrubs were brought here from Asia because of their beauty, but are now considered invasive. Look for their bright pink flowers in spring and their red fruit, called "hips," which look like tomatoes with legs, in late summer and early fall.

The red hip of *Rosa rugosa* >

Firm russula mushroom

Find this large yellowish mushroom hanging out under the conifers in summer and fall. It's so big you can use pebbles to make art on it. I found one with a chunk taken out of it and made Pac-Man. What can you make from the shape you found? Take a whiff—it smells pretty fishy.

< A *Russula compacta* Pac-Man

FROLIC THROUGH FERNALD'S NECK PRESERVE

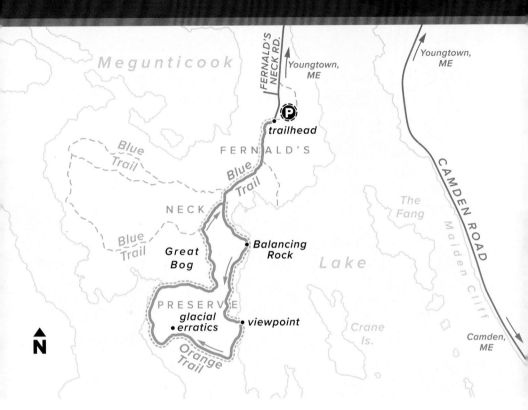

YOUR ADVENTURE

Adventurers, are you ready to explore a bog? This wet, spongy ground is on the historic homeland of the Wabanaki. In 1969, a developer had plans to build here, but a group of local residents purchased the land and made it a trust instead. It is named for the narrow strip of land you'll cross, the "neck," and for Allen and Sally Fernald, who made their own conservation

LENGTH

2.6-mile

lollipop loop

250–

ELEV [FT]

Elevation Gain

125–

115ft.

1   2   3   4

DISTANCE [MI]

HIKE + EXPLORE 1.5 hours

DIFFICULTY Moderate—up and down, but fairly short and plenty to see

SEASON Year-round. Best May to October.

GET THERE From Camden, take ME-52 / Mountain Street north and turn left on Fernald's Neck Road. It ends at the parking lot in 1 mile.

Google Maps: bit.ly/timberfernalds

RESTROOMS At parking lot

FEE None

TREAT YOURSELF Never say no to a good general store, especially one only 3 miles away. Brick-oven pizza and tons of fun local goodies await at Lincolnville Center General Store on Main Street Lincolnville.

Coastal Mountains Land Trust
(207) 236-7091
Instagram @Coastal_Mountains_Land_
Trust | Facebook @CoastMountainsLT

Power up on the shore
of Megunticook Lake

gift—the summit of Bald Mountain, which you can see to the southeast. Start in a lovely meadow and go straight on the Blue Trail, then dip into the needle-carpeted forest with Megunticook Lake (meaning "great swells of the sea" in the Penobscot language) on your left as you take the Orange Trail to Balancing Rock. Pass by a tree's uprooted rootball and stop for power-ups at two beautiful lakeside spots. When you reach Balancing Rock, power up on the chairlike rock nearby, then continue on, passing footbridges and a couple glacial boulders until you reach the Great Bog. Turn right at the Blue Trail to make your way back to the start.

SCAVENGER HUNT

Balancing Rock and lichen
The Laurentide Ice Sheet left this glacial erratic balancing in what looks like a precarious position. Have your buddy take a picture of you pretending to knock it over. Examine it for lichen, which can be crusty, leafy, or bushy. What kinds can you find?

< Look closely at the lichen on the rocks around you

Deer mushroom
Look for these fungi breaking down wood. How many do you see clustered around each other? If you can get your nose up close for a sniff, you'll smell their special radishy smell. Can you count high enough to count all the gills on one mushroom?

Pluteus cervinus >

Bald eagle

Look for these national symbols by the water's edge. Make sure to stay still and try to wait at least five minutes, concentrating on the trees and the sky as you look for them. In 1972, Maine had only twenty-seven nesting pairs. Today, there are over 700. Look up high in trees for their giant nests, called aeries (*air*-ees).

Haliaeetus leucocephalus (in Greek, *leuco* means "white" and *cephalus* means "head") ∧

Great Bog

A bog is a wet, spongy environment where years and years of peat moss have built up and created a unique ecosystem. The soil here stays wet and doesn't have a lot of nutrients, so only specially adapted plants can grow. Do you think you have what it takes to grow in a bog?

< Approach the bog before the end of your journey

American bittern

This bog dweller's booming call is often mistaken for a bullfrog's. To feed, it stands still in the water, camouflaged among the reeds, and waits for prey—fish, eels, snakes, frogs—to approach. Then it strikes quickly with its sharp bill. Play bittern tag—one person stands straight up, swaying back and forth like a reed, while the other sees how close they can get before the bittern strikes.

Botaurus lentiginosus is a type of heron >

ACKNOWLEDGMENTS

New England is a magical and huge place, filled with generous folks all passionate about conservation, outdoors, and families. Many an email, call, clarification, and reclarification was shared as we dug up old photos with the local historical society or looked closely at photos of rocks found on the trail. I'm so happy to include their names here, but I wish I could do more! Huge thanks to Gregg Mangan, Connecticut Humanities; Alan Levere, Connecticut Department of Energy and Environmental Protection; Walter Woodward, University of Connecticut and State Historian; Cynthia Fowx, The Nature Conservancy; Scott Santino, Mass Audubon; Kim Calcagno and Laura Carberry, Audubon Society of Rhode Island; Tiffany Link, Maine Historical Society; Jim Thompson, Mount Tom Reservation; Darren Ranco, University of Maine; Robert Marvinney, Maine State Geologist; Steve Mabee, Massachusetts State Geologist; John Dickerman and Erik Nelson, New Hampshire State Parks; Corinne Waite; Jane Sawyers, Rhode Island Department of Environmental Management; Stephen Perkins, Vermont Historical Society; Dr. Mauri Pelto; Dan Tinkham, Belknap Range Trail Tenders; Geralyn Ducady, Rhode Island Historical Society; Lorén Spears, Tomaquag Museum; Andrea Masisak, Connecticut Department of Energy and Environmental Protection; Paul Grant-Costa, Yale University; Randolph Steinen; Lance Hansen, CFPA Walcott Blue-Blaze Trail Manager; Jeanne Ammermuller, Redding Land Trust; Julie Judkins, Appalachian Trail Conservancy; Danna Strout, Green Mountain National Forest, Manchester ranger District; Nancy Jones, Bradford Conservation Commission; Ethan Phelps, Vermont State Parks; Chris Silsbee, Bradbury Mountain State Park; Bill Patterson, The Nature Conservancy; Kenneth Norden, Forest Service; Richard Moore, Pulpit Rock Subcommittee, Bedford Conservation Commission; Adam Moore, Sheriff's Meadow Foundation;

Rick Blanchette, Friends of the Wapack; Lisa Wright, State of Vermont Department of Forest, Parks, and Recreation; Bob Spoerl and Scott Rolfe, New Hampshire Department of Natural and Cultural Resources; Brad Greenough and Walter Opuszynski, State of Vermont Department of Forests, Parks, and Recreation; Jim Armbruster, Vermont Institute of the Natural Sciences; Jon Kim and Marjorie Gale, Vermont State Geologists.

Huge thanks to Stacee Lawrence, Cobi Lawson, Mike Dempsey, Katlynn Nicolls, Sarah Crumb, Sarah Milhollin, and the entire Timber Press family for believing in this newest guide for New England families. And to "Map Master" David Deis for his beautiful work.

And to my family—to Gail, Xavier, and Jaedon Moore for being my trusty guinea pigs, to my father, Alan, for being an amazing driver and hiker, to my husband, Garrison, for being head GPS tracker and cheerleader and chef, and to my mother, Ginny, for her research, driving, and time-keeping and safety skills. This book is about family, and support from a strong family makes adventure possible.

And thanks to all of you for reading this and getting outside with each other! I can't wait to see the adventures you go on.

PHOTO AND ILLUSTRATION CREDITS

All photos by the author or her father, Alan Gorton, except the following:

INDEX

ABOUT YOUR LEAD ADVENTURER

Wendy holds a master's degree in learning technologies and is a former classroom teacher. As part of her quest to bring science education to life, she worked as a National Geographic Fellow in Australia researching Tasmanian devils, a PolarTREC teacher researcher in archaeology in Alaska, an Earthwatch teacher fellow in the Bahamas and New Orleans, and a GoNorth! teacher explorer studying climate change via dogsled in Finland, Norway, and Sweden. Today, she is a global education consultant who has traveled to more than fifty countries to design programs, build communities, and inspire other educators to do the same. She enjoys mountain biking, rock climbing, kayaking, backpacking, yoga, photography, traveling, writing, and hanging out with her family and nephews. Follow her on social media @50hikeswithkids and email wendy@50hikeswithkids.com.